READING HISTORICAL DOC~~UMENTS~~

A manual for students

READING HISTORICAL DOCUMENTS

A manual for students

John Fines

Basil Blackwell

For Frances, at last

First published 1988
© John Fines 1988

Published by Basil Blackwell Limited
108 Cowley Road
Oxford OX4 1JF
England

British Library Cataloguing in Publication Data

Fines, John
  Reading historical documents: a manual
  for students.
  1. Historiography
  I. Title
  907 D13

  ISBN 0–631–90167–1

Typset in 11/13 pt Palatino
by Opus, Oxford
Printed in Great Britain by Page Bros, Norwich

The cover photograph shows 'Clever Hans', a horse reputed to be able to read, perform calculations, spell and understand musical intervals, in Berlin c1900. Hans and his owner, Carl von Osten, were the subject of many tests by animal psychologists, who eventually concluded that the horse was responding to unconscious 'signals' from its owner.

Contents

Do documents really matter?

Akhmatova wrote a preface to the poem, which reads: 'I spent 17 months in prison queues waiting for news in those years of the Yezhovschina' – the Russian word for the purges, after Nikolai Yezhov, who commanded the NKVD secret police until he himself became a victim in 1939 – she begins.

'Once somebody identified me and picked me out. And a woman in the queue behind me, her lips blue, standing with that rigidity we all shared, whispered to me. We all whispered in those days. She did not know my name, but she asked: 'Can you ever describe this?'

'"I can", I said, and there appeared what might have been a smile on what used to be her face.'

The *Guardian* 21.3.87

Introduction

This book is addressed in the first instance to students. It works in the way I teach, and uses the language and the techniques I use in teaching. It isn't formal and some might say it isn't very logical; all I can say is, it works.

You, the student, can read this book on your own and work at the exercises on your own if that suits you best, but the intention is that this should be a class manual, with a teacher working alongside students, and lots of discussion taking place. I know that you will be on your own in the exam room, and that you will have to work at speed, but in class you are preparing for this, not living it through; there is a difference, so take your time, work slowly and carefully and stop to talk a lot– you will find it excellent preparation.

I haven't set out to choose documents that 'fit' any particular syllabus – if I did it would have taken dozens of books, and I don't think they would have helped you in the end. The examples I am using are rather more interesting than those you will find on the exam papers, and better for practice. If you conscientiously follow through the course established here you will be ready to answer any of the various examination papers' document questions, and you will have learned en route a lot about how historians use evidence, and why.

This programme is in steps, and your teacher might like to review the whole programme first to sort out the right pace to take the steps. It may be that you will want to try the steps in bits and pieces, coming back to them from time to time, or you might like to go through the whole lot thoroughly in one fell swoop. My preference would be for the first strategy, but you must consider your circumstances.

Remember that every examination board gives at least a fifth of its marks for document questions in 'A' level history, so whatever course you are doing, this will be relevant. So let's waste no more time and get straight down to work, asking the first question:

1

What is a document?

When we say we are 'doing History', at whatever level, we have to be aware that there are three constituents to this process:

1 the past itself;

2 the source materials left behind by the past and kept until our times, available to us for use;

3 the histories historians (which includes us) write.

This might seem to you a rather fussy distinction, but be patient and you will see that understanding it is the very essence of understanding your subject.

First of all, then, the past. Now we know it happened (unless we are a very funny kind of philosopher, and let's take it for the time being that we are not). The sad thing is that we can never know for sure anything about it, because we cannot go back into the past to check it. A scientist can re-run an experiment as many times as he or she likes, to make assurance doubly sure, but we historians can't have even one re-run. We can *agree* on some things simply because everyone else says it is so, and there is no sense in challenging the 'fact'. For example, we accept that the Battle of Hastings took place in 1066 because everyone says it did and there is no reason to doubt it – to disagree simply wouldn't get us anywhere. We can also *guess* about the past, basing our guesswork on logic, common sense and our experience of how people behave in general. We can guess, for example, that William's victory at Hastings was a bit of a surprise event, brought about by the feigned retreat and leaving the Normans so shaken that they sat about for a week not too sure what to do next. We can guess that, but we can't be certain. Our knowledge is *provisional* knowledge, in that it might have to change. That sounds rather deflating, but think for a minute about the scientists, who *can* check – they are always changing their minds. Ask a physicist to explain about the nature of matter – is it a particle or a wave? Or both? Or one at one time, the other at another? Why is Einstein now 'wrong'? Red faces all round.

Historians, when they tell the story of the past, or explain how it happened (which can mean the same thing), are giving their *versions* of history, ones which they have themselves constructed. Now historians come in all shapes and types – some sloppy, some careful, some imaginative, some pedestrian, some fair and honest in their intentions, some less so. And all of them are shaped by their own backgrounds, the times they live in, the values they hold, their beliefs about society and the subtle things that have gone into shaping them as human beings.

Let me give you a personal example (it will save me being sued by other historians). I wrote my first major historical study for a PhD degree; it had to be submitted to an examiner who was an expert in the field. The subject was medieval heretics, those people who opposed the views of the universal church and got persecuted for it. Now I came from a working-class background, and had been brought up to go to an evangelical church which had taught me that all forms of religious ceremonial and control were bad. I didn't continue to be a member of that church (or chapel, to be correct) and had for many years thought of myself as an agnostic, a non-believer, but it did strike me that I was likely, with this background, to be on the side of the heretics, and so I should be *very* careful in what I wrote. Now, when the examiner came to tell me I had got the PhD he put on a serious face (of course he had not met me before the examination, and knew nothing of my background). He sternly warned me that those Roman Catholic historians who allowed their faith to influence what they wrote were falling into a dangerous trap, and that I should watch my step. I had, in fact, leaned over backwards so much to be fair to the other side, that, instead of favouring the heretics, my dissertation favoured the Church. I'm afraid to say that the formal examination degenerated into laughter all round.

So how can we control this wild animal of history, with a past we can't know, and utterly unreliable historians intruding their personal biases (whether known or subconscious) in all directions? The only hope we have, and that a small one, is constituent 2 – the source materials. Unfortunately, they themselves present a whole load of problems, and this book is designed to help you make your first steps in dealing with them.

In Britain we are surrounded by survivals from the past, so much so

3

that visitors consider us as just 'cute' antiques. Visit a 'new' country like the USA and you will find that things which we see as commonplace are to them unique 'survivals'. This is a good point to start at, for sources are survivals and we need to consider how they survived. Source materials from the past face a lot of dangers; let's make a list.

- *fire* – very common in a wood-building age, and still a problem in ours

- *damp* – water destroys paper very fast indeed and acid-bearing damp is fastest. Victorian books are decaying on our shelves today

- *rats, mice, insects* – yuk, let's not think of them too much, but the first major record office I worked in was so infested that you heard a distinct rustle every time you entered a store room

- *people who throw things away* – I, yes I am one of these. My waste paper basket is always full, I am always throwing things out, mainly because I would become overwhelmed with paper if I didn't

- *developers* – people who see other uses for old things that survive and are in their way. These people are everywhere, and they need opposing, for they are only after money

Just as much of a problem are the people who save things – people we might think are on our side. We need to know *why* things have survived, so that we can know their significance. Earlier this century there was, for example, a great collector of *ephemera*, called John Johnson – his collection is now in the Bodleian Library at Oxford. He collected – get ready for it – RUBBISH! Anything anyone threw away or discarded – regarded as worthless – he put into his collection. It is a marvellous archive, but it represents the sort of things archaeologists commonly deal with – the *least* important things of our lives . . . Or does it?

We must be aware of how sources come to us, why they have survived. In my work, for example, I deal with heretics, but I only know them because they appear in court records that have survived. What about the heretics who never came to court? Am I not dealing with the accident-prone, loud-mouthed individuals who actually got taken up and prosecuted? What about the wise heretics who kept a low profile? Well we have no sources that deal with them.

4

So, when we approach a document we must be very careful. We must ask a number of searching questions:

1 Who wrote this?

2 Why? For what purpose?

3 When? In what circumstances?

4 To whom?

5 What other things do I need to know about those circumstances to understand what is going on here?

You may well need to do a lot of checking up. You might need to read biographies of the people concerned (the *Dictionary of National Biography* is a work to consult first). You might need to find out about the times and the places, to consult a Chronology and an Historical Atlas. Working with documents requires a great deal of checking up. You might well need to consult a Dictionary to see what a specific word or phrase meant at that time, for in the past people spoke and wrote differently.

Be ready, be prepared, to be
                    An HISTORIAN –

How to tackle a document in eight easy steps

There is no golden road to anything really, but the best advice I can give you is to split up your task in such a way as to move steadily towards your objective, and not to try to go too fast when you are just practising. I know you will need to perform at speed in the examination hall, and later on you will have to practise working at speed, but first take slow steps in an orderly fashion.

Step one is to describe your document (very much as I was indicating at the end of the last section). What is it – a letter, a diary, an official form, a newspaper article? Is it personal and private or official and public? Where does it come from, how did it survive? All these small questions will set your mind at work about the document and will give you the chance to scan it several times. The *worst* way to try to tackle a document is to try to read it word by word, line by line. You will only get depressed that way, convinced that you don't understand half the words, that the task is too hard. Let your eyes scamper over it several times, glancing through and ignoring all the difficult bits at first, just familiarising yourself with the shape of it.

Then when you have had a few brief rushes over the surface of the document, write a brief description of it, as if you were a librarian or an archivist writing a catalogue card for it. Never mind how rough your version is – 'some bloke seems worried about a fire or something, in America, I think, in about 1890, or perhaps not, and it is to do with cotton or cloth (maybe)'. Then compare what you have got with others in the class, and discuss it.

Now you are ready for *step two* which is purely mechanical and calls for little brain power in the first instance. You need to split up all the separate pieces of information the document contains and put them under headings of some sort. I often work at this stage with just four headings:

- information about *people*

6

- information about *time*

- information about *places*

- information about *ideas*

You may find that the document you are working on throws up different headings from these, and maybe many more, but try not to let the headings get out of hand – when you have had your first go at it, come back to see whether you can cut the number of headings down. Again, this is a good thing to discuss in class.

Step three is all about ignorance, which is no disgrace so long as you admit it. Go through the document and underline everything you don't understand or things that could do with looking up (as I said on page 5) in a dictionary, chronology, atlas, biographical dictionary or textbook. Make a habit of looking things up. I know you will be thinking 'The fool has forgotten we can't take books into the exam' but I do remember, and deplore that. If in practice you concentrate on what you don't understand and can look up, you *will* be wiser when you are on your own in the exam hall. I promise you. And on the paper they do explain *very* difficult items (usually).

Step four is a tricky one. Read the document again (by the time you have finished these scans of the text you will know it backwards!) to see how much it is a product of its own times. People think, behave and write differently in different periods of history, and we need to notice that before we can assess the significance of what is being said. So make a short list of the things in the document that mark its period – I don't mean dates nor the 'yeas' and 'hereinuntos' but the *attitudes*. I *know* it is hard, but remember you are at step four.

Step five follows on from that, and is all about the trust you would place in what is being said, about the reliability of the source. Does it betray biases, hidden assumptions, points of view that affect the evidence? Does it miss out significant things that you might have expected *should* be there? List these and discuss them. At this stage start to use examples of phraseology from the document – which words or phrases make you suspect something, and why. *Always* give your reasons, however fluffy they may sound. It is perfectly fair for you to say 'The way he talks makes me think he is a creep', but you must show why.

Step six is to think very hard about what questions the document raises in your mind (and again this is best done in discussion).

Remember that history is all about speculation (whatever some exam boards say, they don't matter here) and you must learn to speculate as proper historians do. They come away from a document saying 'I just wonder whether . . .?' and so must you. What directions of enquiry does your document point to? Imagine the document was the very start of a long research process, lasting several years and ending up in a book. What questions would be the foundation of that book?

Step seven involves deciding the importance, the significance of your document. It is rather more than just what the document means, it is about how the document might be used by an historian. What could it prove? What is it worth (not in money, but in history)? Is it vital, or just a side issue? Is there more in it than meets the eye?

Step eight is often ignored, but it is important for people who will end up in exam rooms. How are you going to record all your findings? If you have been obedient you will have accumulated endless bits of scribble about the document by now, you will have had stiff debates with all your colleagues. Now how does that become a statement about the document – tight, crisp, clear and accurate, but also an honest and full record of your feelings? Think hard on this one and try lots of drafts – again work with colleagues drafting out ideas . . . (Yes I know you can't collude in the exam hall, more's the pity, but there's nothing to stop you now.)

Scanning and analysis

I am starting you off on the two most difficult documents of the whole collection. What a pig I am! But I have chosen them so that you have something to bite on. You need to practise scanning difficult materials to give you confidence when you approach the easier examples given in the exam hall.

There are two documents to work on, with different kinds of difficulty to overcome (although they share the difficulty of considerable length.) The first is in two parts (with a small addition which is really just for fun): the first section dates from 1682 and is a portion of Hugh Squiers' draft plan for setting up a school at South Molton in Devonshire. The second dates from 1693 and is a letter from Squiers about a new teacher for the school. I have typed it up just as I found it – spelling and punctuation unchanged, so you *should* have some difficulty reading it; if you don't, there is something wrong!

The task here is to list evidence contained in the sources about attitudes to education at the end of the seventeenth century. Set out your list under headings of your own. Itemise all the evidence, but try to keep your headings under control – don't have too many.

A second task is to see whether Squiers' opinions have changed in the ten years or so that separate the two documents. No clues on offer, find out for yourself.

The second document, one long letter, comes from a more recent period, 1959. Its special difficulty is that it hasn't been transcribed into print, but is left in the original handwriting. It was written by Kenneth Kaunda, leader of Zambia today; it records the full details of his arrest by the British authorities. Your job is to list, under headings, *all* the evidence it contains about the behaviour of British administrators and their colonial subjects in the very last stage of the British Empire. Remember, you are not a politician, but a dispassionate historian – list all the evidence, good and bad.

. . . And this shall not be an horne book schooll, to learn little children to read, nor shall any one be admitted but such as can read in the psalter before they are admitted, nor shall it be only to teach persons the Latin tongue or the rules of Grammer, But this school shall be chiefly to teach good writing and Arithmetick. Arithmetick as necessary as our dayly bread, as salt unto our meat, the thing which every man is making use of, every houre of all his life, if that he be awake, for want whereof some persons who are poor mistake in thinking they are rich, and others who are Rich, mistake and think that they are poor. What better knowledge than for a man to know himself, which cannot be done in any tollerable measure without this art so necessary both by sea and land, no man can go to sea without it and at land, a man will badly thrive who can't make up a reckoning of what he doth, nothing more necessary to every ones prosperity than to be able to use his pen. And therefore whyles others build Almeshouses to relieve the poor I do design to prevent them from ever being poor and instead of living in others Almeshouses, that some of these may build in my name Almeshouses for others to live in. And besides this usefulness and proffit, the very ornament and pleasure thereof is not inconcidered. How ignoble is it, for one to pretend to be a gentleman in his family, and a clowne in his educacion a thing too common (in our parts of the Kingdome) for want of worthy schools to Nourture youth And how much our youth hath been abused, and cheated of thys pretious thing called tyme, I have bin too much a witnes of, and it hath offerd me matter of compassion these many years. To see the godly good old wife (in the middest of all her other pressing Affairs) take pains to pack her boyes away to Schooll (becaus shee thinks tis for thyr good) there to learne not to read divinity nor so much as history, nor the tale of Tom Thumb which would prove to be farr more proffitable than some horum harum horum, genitivo hujus dubito huic &c wen she is sure she can mayntaine them but 2 years at the schooll, in all, by which means all her cost and pains and tyme so pretious tyme is lost, lyke dictates written on the sand, Yea (without hyperboly) quite so much lost as her owne husbands labour would be, if hee should burne & lymbe & dung and plow his land when he fore knows he can never live to sowe it. I say either go on and perfect Grammer with the latin tongue or else tis madnes to begin for unles a man meanes to be a divine or a lawyer or an apothecary or a gentleman hee makes no use thereof but forgetts again all that he learnt, and is not much the wiser man if that he could remember it still. I appeall to all the impericall men who shall live in many ages after I am dead and gone whether this our way of learning grammer for 2 or 3 years and no more be a proper and an wholesome way of entring & educating such youths as are to get thyr livings in the world and I appeall unto our present age whether there be any beauty in't to let a shoemaker or suchlike handicraftsman brag that hee hath bin 2 year at the Grammer schooll and throw some shred of falce latin up and down, where it becomes him like a saddle on a sow, an ignorant parriting man, a beggar proud. And this poor man can hardly write his name when called to be a witnes to a lease which gives the lie to all his pretennes of being a learned schollar in his youth.

And therefor, and becaus there are enough of them elsewhere, I do ordain that this shall be no Grammer schooll, but some what more proffitable to those that intend to prospere in the world and I do recommend that the school master shall teach that gentyle character which is in use amonge secratarys of corn or other merchants in most marityne townes, and also court hand that they may be able to read a writt them selves, and also Arithmetick, and that in fractions to, and I would also have a chapter in the old testament, & a psalme or some convenient part thereof read every forenoon with a gloria patri, and then proceed unto their work, and also a chapter of the new testament with detto psalme and gloria patria (sic) every afternoon, before they do begin thyr work, which may be read perhaps by one of the schollars of the schooll . . .'

15 February 1693

Yesterday I received 2 letters from Mr Mallaree and from his son And formerly I have had severall Applications from a pretended scholler in Exon an other from Mr Beare who is Burgis in Parliament for Tyverton in behalf of a Clergie man &c. I tould him for Answer that I had the choyce of severall heer, particularly Mr More the writing schole master in King Street who hath now above 60 boys in his schole, Besides his going home to great mens houses where he taught all the Marquess of Carmarthen's Children, hee taught my owne children & I have been Witnes to his good life and conversacion about 20 years, and he would gladly go from hence and teach at Molton. But I must rob Peter to pay Paul nor disfurnish this place to enrich S. Molton. I did not think there had been so silly a cocks comb in England as he that wroat to me from Exon, my Footboy can outdo him in his owne Trade. But Mr Bear's clergie man & my cousin Gibbons Friend have had their Answers. Yeaven a French Begger at my dore pretended he could teach to Philosophy. The world is full of cheats and there seldom comes a better – the Faults of one we know, but we do not know the faults of another Mr Heele (now heer) importuned me to turn my schole into a Grammar schole, that so his Children & other Gentry might be taught it at home. I answered let his (and anybodys Children with all my heart) learn there to write &c. Nor would I hinder young Mallaree (for the tyme present) from teaching such the beginnings of the Grammar too – But tis in hopes that he will never let it grow to be a comon latin schole, for then my Charity would be abused, my designe defeated, and all my cost and labour lost. I hardly know any thin more nauceous than to see a Begger Proud or to hear a cobler boast of some few shred of latin which he hath gott by the end and thinks that makes him a gentleman when it becomes him like a sylken saddle upon a sow, which will never grow to be a race horse. And most comonly those boys will have a soft place in their head when they are grown men & the reason thereof is they were so Busyed about their horum harum horum That they had no tyme to think and then it follows that they must be fooiis. And when the good old wife hath kept her biggest boy to the Latin schole and seen him whipt some tymes, then all must needs bee well: tho the thing so learnt bee no better than perfect Poyson unto his intellectualls and the best yeares tyme most miserably mispent. I have bin greeved to see my Countrymen so much abused for I love the place of my Nativity and the very ground of the place and the people that go upon the ground and the chieff good I can do them is to help them that they may not mispend their pretious tyme.

I have observed that scholemasters are most comonly the proudest of men, perhaps their constant domineering over their boys may be the cause of it. But old Mr Mallarree is not so. I have the best letter from him that ever was writt to any body. And the man hath so much good Nature as to proffet that hee will bestow a good loud sounding clock, and fix it on the schole, and also will set up a sundyall and will pave the way between Mr Rudge his ground and ours, and will make out a little dore to the upper corner of the house of Office, and will furnish the poorer children with paper pen and Inke and will give them a Feast when the governors have their feast, all which I take very kindly at his hand, and look on it as a great prooff of his honesty and fair dealing &c. And therfor I make it my Request to you that his son may succeed his father . . .'

Devon R.O. TD. 81.

If you doubt Mr Squiers' complaints about applicants for school masters' posts, you might like to read the following . . .

Biccer Brige Dec.r = 28 = 1819

Honnered Sir I Receved your kind Letter and heit his Ben of Gret Sarves to me at theis present tim for I vas vere neadfull of a frind at the present tim. I went and Bought Joseph lancaster Buck of derictons for teaicheng the naitonall scool and the spalling By thought By Do.r Bell of Madrass and I heave Bein studing theit Ever Sin I Bought heit But I Could not dou at your loge without further support than I have at prisint for ther is vere fou Children at Grimston I might teach = 100 = Children By his Derictons as Easey as tann I leve my salf to you Good Gugiment and frindship What Wold Be the Beast for me for to Dou

    John Fraser

East Riding Record Office, DDGR 43/39

HOW I WAS ARRESTED

On the 12th day of March, 1959 and at about 1 a.m. I heard a knock at the door. Of hut no. 257 chilenje which I occupy but belongs to the Lusaka Municipal Council.

In response I said, "Hellow, who is there?" The reply was, "POLICE,". "Yes, what can I do for you?" I went on. Someone growled back commandingly, "OPEN." I then said, "Just a minube please," After a few seconds someone started beating at the door. My wife got annoyed and said "Mispana Uwaka matiseche?" (which means literally "Do you want us to get up naked?") The drumming went on until the two pairs of scissors — which I had pushed in the staple before repairing to bed — gave way & the next thing I saw was a pair of policemen — one in uniform — the other one in plain clothes — right inside my bedroom. I was just completing dressing.

The uniformed policeman came nearer & told me to pack one suitcase only. As I was packing the plain cloth man was also busy removing my books, files & other papers. and for the first time I noticed two other policemen both in plain clothes — one was black & the other was white.

13

Soon after I had packed the man in uniform came up to me and producing some papers and carefully concealing them leaned on my narrow shelf and commanded me to attach my signature in a specially marked place. After I had done as he had commanded he quickly slipped them back into what seemed to be a pocket inside his jersey. It could have been his shirt pocket I am not sure.

After this he handcuffed my left hand against the right hand of the African police man + then addressing me said, "I hope that won't be necessary." I made no reply. He turned to my wife and told her to report to the District Commissioner in the morning.

Outside I saw a net-wired jeep + for the first time I realised where my silent-working police friends were taking my books, files + papers. We had to step on them to occupy our seats but they were so full the uniformed policeman, who apparently was in command, ordered the black policeman to occupy one of the front seats. This left room for the owner's gunner of the two plain clothe white men. He sat near me on my right + my right hand was handcuffed against his left. So I sat between them two men handcuffed despite the fact that I had offered no resistance.

The junior of these plain clothes white officers flashed a bright torch light at my wife's face who was by now standing near the kitchen door which had also been forced open by them. I said, "Hallo, why?" He switched off.

From here they drove me to the Woodlands Police Post. I heard one of them say the time was 1.30 a.m. The fellow who was in charge addressing the white chaps to whom I was handcuffed said, "I won't be long ......" The man addressed replied, "How do you mean you won't be long?" disapprovingly. When he came back he was carrying something + together they made a finger print of my right thumb on one of the pages of their copious papers.

We went past the Government House, the Secretariat + on to King George Avenue, Cairo Road + finally took the Broken Hill road. We didn't stop until we had gone past the Lusaka Municipal Boundary. At a certain point we turned left and after a few yards we halted. They unhandcuffed me + handed me to a van amidst about a dozen police jeeps + cars.

me were scores of armed police men. Then
came Mr Seed. He said, "Yes, Kaunda I
was to come at 8 o'clock but I changed my
mind & came earlier." I just looked at him.
& said nothing.   Before getting into the
van they searched me & got away my diary.
In the van I found Mr Kapwepwe, treasurer
of Zambia & Mr Kapwepolo another Zambia
man. Later Messrs John Mwashi & Chipone
Lusaka district leaders joined us. My suitcase
was then brought and just opposite the rear
van door they started searching my clothes.
They threw them around on wet ground
carelessly. I complained but those officers who
stood round just laughed at me.

At a later stage, Mr Chipano got pressed &
asked to be taken outside where he could
relieve himself. He was told to help himself
at the door of the van while they ran round
laughing at him. I also wanted to help
myself but demanded privacy for such business
for I could not help myself with scores of
policemen watching. They laughed back and
one of them said that if I could not help
myself then it was my own look out.

After this episode I made an attempt

to find out where we were going. I said
addressing my friends, "I am glad I am
going to see my mother at last." One of
the officers sitting in front laughed & said,
"You will be sorry my friend. You are going
in an entirely opposite direction." This is all
I managed to work out of them.

Round about 4.30 am we drove towards
Broken Hill closely followed by a jeep. After a
few miles we drove back to Lusaka and stopped
at the police post near the Central African
Road Services offices. A few moments later we
drove on this time led by a police car, &
followed by a jeep. We took the Fort Johnson
round. Branching off we made for the Government
House & then for the Hospital roundabout,
followed a road that led us into the airport.
We went round & round & then went straight
to the airport where we found a plane ready
to take off. Here we found scores more of
police men. These were even more heavily
armed than those I have described earlier.

Our van stopped very near the plane.
Two hefty fellows came forward to take me to
the plane. They stretched my arms to the mail & —
with palms facing the stars in the sky — in

such a way that I thought my elbows had been broken.

Once aboard the plane things changed. For the first time that morning I came across a kindly police officer. He told us he was not authorised to tell us where we were going but that Mr Kapongolu would remain at our first station of calling.

Our first station was Ndola. Our colleague remained but we were joined by six more. Messrs Hyden Banda (Ndola), Jonathan Chivatya, (Ndola), Naphas Tembo (Ndola), Joseph Lucas Munlenga (Ndola), Kapangala (Nchanga) & Ralph Kombe (Broken Hill). Here, we were offered dry biscuits + corned beef.

Here again I asked to go and help myself. When a constable followed me I protested. I was told by the officer that that was the order. He added in one and half hours' time we would be reaching our next station where I was remaining & so may be I could hang on. I did.

The next station was Balovale + here Ralph Kombe + I remained. The white men with a number of messengers met us + they drove us to the District Commissioner's office. After meeting the District Commissioner I was taken between two officers to an house shared by two district officers where after lunch I was told I was still going ahead. On asking where I was going they told me they were not authorised to tell me.

At about 2, a government entomologist was asked to give me a lift. On the way he told me he had been asked to give me a lift up to Kabompo. Apparently, he had not been tipped not to tell me & so for the first time the mask was off but I had only about 20 miles to go. We reached Kabompo at about 6 p.m.

About 10 minutes later Mr Chitabule from Fort Jameson also arrived brought by one of the district officers at Belmole.

The District Commissioner told us he would give each one of us 3/- per day. I told him my normal diet in Lusaka does not cost less than 15/- per day. I suggested that in the circumstances the government should keep the money & provide for our daily needs. This 3/- was later raised to 4/6 per day each.

On the 24th day of March the District officer Mr MISDEN A. McINNES

served me with a restriction ordered
purported to have come from the Governor
of Northern Rhodesia, Sir Arthur Benson.

Since my arrival here I have
suffered terribly. During the first week
I was attacked by dysentry. After a
couple of weeks I was attacked by malaria
fever. This was followed by a bad
cold & cough from which I am just
recovering.

I with
K. D. Kaunda

20/4/59

DETAINEES' CAMP,
KABOMPO

A sense of time and period

Look back to what I had to say on page 7 about *Stage 4*. This section is devoted to looking hard at documents in order to get a feel for the times they come from. You could equally well use the first two documents for this exercise, and if you want to practise thorough reading, scanning and re-scanning, it would be wise to do so. But if you feel like a change, try these new ones.

First of all, think about how we represent the past, how we attempt to capture time and a sense of period. Sometimes we do it by telling stories. Sometimes we do it by highlighting the differences between now and then. There are lots of ways of representing this difference. Look at Minard's map of the campaign of 1812 on the next page. How well do you think this works – what are the advantages and disadvantages of showing time in this way? Does it show the difference between now and then? Discuss this in class.

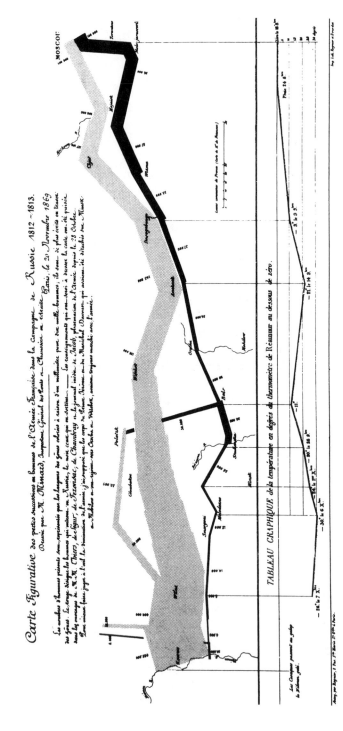

This map, drawn by the French engineer Charles Joseph Minard in 1869, portrays the losses suffered by Napoleon's army in the Russian campaign of 1812. Beginning at the left on the Polish-Russian border near the Niemen, the thick band at the top shows the size of the army (422,000 men) as it invaded Russia in June 1812. The width of the band indicates the size of the army at each position. In September, the army reached Moscow, which was by then sacked and deserted, with 100,000 men. The path of Napoleon's retreat from Moscow in the bitterly cold winter is depicted by the dark lower band, which is tied to a temperature scale (note how the path of retreating army and the temperature line move in parallel). The remains of the Grande Armée struggled out of Russia with only 10,000 men. Minard displayed six dimensions of data on the two-dimensional surface of the paper. It may well be the best statistical graphic ever drawn.

22

Now to a game. The second group of documents are jumbled, and I am simply asking you to put them in order again (and *don't* cheat by looking at the answers first). The important thing is to notice *why* you set them in that order, what criteria you are using. Note these things down as you go along, for discussion later. Also make a list of pieces of evidence that tell us specifically about that period, that define the time.

The advertisements on the following pages are all taken from *The Geographical Magazine*; two come from January 1939, four from June 1939, one from May 1940, four from January 1944 and five from October 1945.

First, set all the documents in chronological order as far as possible, giving your reasons in each case. (When you have finished, you can check with the answers at the back of the book.) Then explain what the documents have to tell us about the lifestyle of the readers of the magazine, how it was changing and the overall effect of the war upon them.

1

From the R.A.F.
" 50% of our Mess smoke
one or other of your
Barneys Brands."

From the Middle
East " I have not come
across a Tobacco with the
same even smoking and
flavour of Barneys."

From the NAVY
" Your Barneys is all that
a pipe-lover could desire
—a delightful Tobacco."

They've spread
the fame of
Barneys

Men like these know what's good!
They *deserve* the best, anyway. From
the Navy, the Army, the Air Force—
and the Merchant Service, come these
letters of thanks and appreciation,
from all over the world.

Barneys is as good a Tobacco as you
will encounter in years of searching—
you will never get Tobacco in finer
condition. Three strengths : Barneys
(medium), Punchbowle *(full strength)*,
Parsons Pleasure *(mild)*, 2/9½d. oz.

- to the ends of all the Earth !

24

Kindly mention THE GEOGRAPHICAL MAGAZINE when replying to Advertisements

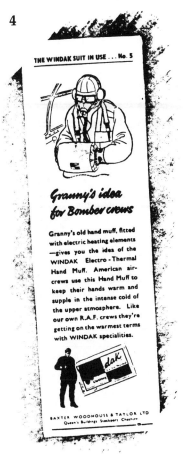
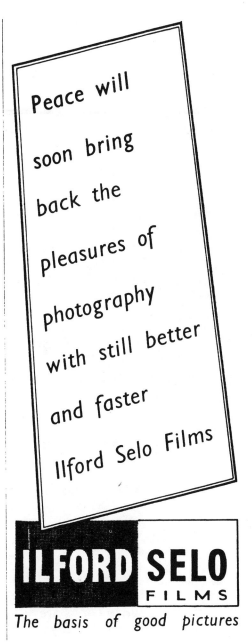

29

ix

i

12

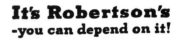
35

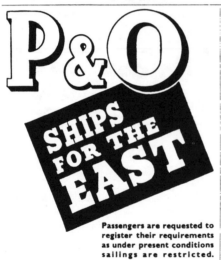

SUPPLIES of 'SANATOGEN' Nerve Tonic are not as plentiful as they were before the war. But it *is* still being made. Ask your chemist for it; even if he cannot supply you immediately, he will be getting his share of 'SANATOGEN' at regular intervals, and will see that you get *your* share.

'SANATOGEN'

Regd. Trade Mark

NERVE TONIC

In one size only—6/6d.

A 'GENATOSAN' Product.

viii

Linia Belts

Customers who need belts for specific health reasons and obtain a certificate from the doctor, can still have the Linia Belt made to their own measurements and requirements. Other wearers should remember that our Wartime Reconditioning Service is still available. But please give us all the time you can.

J. ROUSSEL LTD.

179 REGENT STREET, LONDON, W.I.

Telephone : Reg 7570

And at Birmingham, Glasgow, Liverpool, Manchester, etc.

38

Finally a rather more difficult task. Three fairly recent newspaper clippings. The first two are about a tradition – the past in the present, as it were. The last tells us something about how the past affects the present in a slightly different way, more worryingly, in fact. Discuss the differences between a sense of period (understanding what it was like to live in a different age in the past), the persistence of tradition (continuing the past in the present by habit or inclination), and the influence the past has over us today whether we wish it or no.

Pot hunting: No call

COMMERCIAL Square Bonfire Society, who led this year's United Grand Procession, feel that Bonfire night at Lewes is a great British tradition to be enjoyed without competition and the award of a trophy.

In his bonfire speech the Archbishop, Dr Peter Etherington, said: 'We will accept cups in other areas but Lewes is something very special, a night for pleasure and family fun without the organisation which goes with trying to win awards.

'Commercial Square does not agree with presenting a cup for the best society as it creates ill-feeling and some of the enjoyment of the night is lost.'

Leading the United Grand Procession members of the society immediately attracted attention in their colourful Red Indian and Cowboy costumes.

The initials of the society were held aloft on blazing torches and the Edenbridge Town Band and the TS Valiant NTC Band played rousing music.

The words on their official programme, 'Come ye forth and witness a spectacle the like which ye have often wished for but never seen,' certainly seemed appropriate as they marched down the High Street.

The children loved seeing the destruction of an effigy and a spectacular

firework display. The highlight of the evening was a brilliant tableau of Nelson's Column – it stood 42 feet high – and the Indian's 'Thunder Bird.'

After the fireworks it was the turn of the Mums and Dads to take part in the final ceremony, which closed at Commercial Square with Bonfire Prayers and the singing of 'Rule Britannia' and 'Auld Lang Syne.'

Sussex Express and County Herald
9.11.73

40

On Friday night, as on most Bonfire Nights for 300 years and more, an effigy of a Pope will be paraded through the streets of Lewes in Sussex and taken to a site on the edge of the town where it will be burnt amid general rejoicing. Since the papal belly will be stuffed with fireworks, the demise is likely to be noisy and spectacular.

Not only that but a banner will be prominently displayed carrying the legend 'No Popery', and there will be a solemn recital of what in Sussex is called 'the bonfire prayer'. It begins, familiarly enough, with:
Please remember,
The Fifth of November,
Gunpowder, Treason and Plot
But it continues in more aggressive vein:
A furden (farthing) loaf to feed old Pope,
A pen-worth of cheese to choke him,
A pint o'beer to rense it down,
An' a faggot o'wood to burn him!
Burn him in a tub o'tar,
Burn him like a blazing star,
Burn his body from his head,
Then we'll say old Pope is dead!
Hip, Hip, hoo-r-r-ray.

Jim Etherington, a local schoolmaster who is secretary of Lewes Bonfire Council, defends these rituals as being an integral part of the Bonfire Night tradition in the town and says they have no reference to the present day. Even so, among some members of the Catholic community in Lewes, this attack on their faith is still a sensitive matter.

As long ago as 1970 Lewes Town Council asked all the bonfire groups, or societies, to drop the papal effigy from their November 5 celebrations after the Cliffe Society burnt a Pope outside the Roman Catholic church itself. But two of the five societies, including Cliffe, still do it. At least the figure is filled with fireworks and not, as apparently was the case in the last century, with live tom cats.

The anti-Catholic feeling in Lewes goes back to the reign of Mary Tudor, when 17 Protestant martyrs were burnt at the stake outside the Star Inn. The discovery of the Guy Fawkes plot to blow up King and Parliament on November 5, 1605, was an opportunity to revive old enmities. The Pope whose effigy is used to this day is Paul V, the contemporary of Fawkes and held by some to have been implicated in the plot.

In the early nineteenth century, Bonfire Night in Lewes was an excuse not only to carry on religious demonstrations but for general displays of hooliganism.

In the 1840s although a local magistrate was attacked by a mob of men and boys on November 5 and householders complained about 'riotous and tumultuous' proceedings, the authorities abandoned attempts to suppress the celebrations, instead bonfire societies were formed to ensure that Bonfire Night was conducted in a more orderly fashion. Not until 50 years later, however, after a shop had been razed to the ground, were fireworks, tar barrels and fires removed from the town centre to the safety of fields nearby.

Preparations for Bonfire Night in Lewes go on for two months and more. Each of the societies makes hundreds of torches of tarred rope, wound round sticks and fastened by wire. In 1929, it was reported, no fewer than 100,000 torches were lit during the evening. Elaborate tableaux are created, often on topical themes. For the 1945 victory celebration, the projected execution of Hermann Goering proved a popular subject, while in the late 1950s a November 5 tableau featured two sputniks, one complete with a dog.

Another local speciality is fancy dress, which probably originated as a form of disguise when passions were stronger than they are now. A Bonfire Night procession in Lewes is likely to include Red Indians. Vikings and Zulu chiefs. With the societies currently active, there are five separate celebrations, though all but one, with their bands, come together in a united grand procession that makes its way through the town centre.

Though Lewes and its 'No popery' provides an extreme example, many of the Bonfire Night traditions were established well before 1605. Fireworks are often supposed to have been invented by the Chinese, reaching Europe in the Middle Ages. Certainly they were popular enough under the Tudors for Elizabeth I to appoint a Firemaster of England. The association of Fawkes and his gunpowder plot made fireworks a natural element of November 5 celebrations.

41

Bonfires had been lit around the beginning of November for many centuries before Guy Fawkes, as part of the pagan festivals when evil spirits would be exorcised to mark the onset of winter. Before 1605, the lighting of fires had been part of another seasonal custom, Hallowe'en. Blazing tar barrels have also been a favourite source of fire-making on November 5, the original with the barrels of gunpowder.

The tar barrel tradition has been maintained in its most spectacular form at Ottery St Mary in Devon. Here the barrels are not just rolled but carried in a sort of relay, by men with hands and arms protected by strong sacking. Each man picks up a barrel in turn, runs as far as he can down the street until the heat becomes too much, when another takes over. In time the barrel becomes too hot for anyone to hold and it is left to disappear in flames.

The traditional guy is dressed in black, holds three fuses in one hand and carries a lantern in the other. Two places where guys are not burned are the Yorkshire village of Scotton, near Knaresborough, where Fawkes lived, and St Peter's, in York, his old school.

Bonfire Night has had its less bloodthirsty aspects. The ringing of church bells was a seasonal ritual from Cornwall to Yorkshire, either on the day itself, known as Ringing Day or on November 4, Ringing Night. And among the sweetmeats made for, and eaten on, November 5, two based on oatmeal, butter and treacle are famous beyond the areas where they originated.

One is parkin, associated particularly with the West Riding of Yorkshire (as was); so much so that in Leeds and elsewhere November 5 has been known as Parkin Day. The other is the thar or tharf cake made in south Yorkshire, Lancashire and Derbyshire. Like other Bonfire Night traditions, it probably goes back well before 1605, one theory being that early November coincides with a feast held in honour of the Scandinavian god, Thor.

The Times 30.10.82

'Burn Catholics' councillor may bow out

Mr George Seawright, a Democratic Unionist member of the Northern Ireland Assembly who was suspended from his party because he called for Catholics and their priests to be incinerated, is expected to withdraw from politics rather than retract.

Mr Seawright, aged 34, who represents North Belfast on both the city council and at Stormont, made the comment last month at a meeting of the Belfast Education and Library Board.

The party's assembly group had withdrawn the Whip from Mr Seawright but his suspension from party membership came on Saturday.

The Times 2.7.84

The Times 2.7.84

Critical reading

Who is right, which version shall I take?

There are four sets of documents in this unit, all presenting a different aspect of the problem facing the historian when he or she has to choose between alternative versions of one subject.

The first set (on pages 44–46) is really designed to show you how the past can deceive (or attempt to deceive) the present. We all know about the dreadful conditions in the Victorian school Dotheboys Hall because Dickens did some investigative journalism and exposed it in *Nicholas Nickleby*. Then, as at all times when shocking things are suddenly revealed, people said 'How were we kept in the dark for so long about this, why didn't we know?' Well, read the first group of documents and find out.

Second, on pages 47–49 there are two contrasting views of pre-First World War Russia, one from Trotsky at his trial, one from the biographer of the Tsar. Read both of them carefully, and *don't* make up your mind in advance. Which of the two versions seems to you to be more correct, and why? If you trust one or both of them, say what in the document(s) gives you confidence: if you distrust, say what rouses your suspicions.

The third group of documents (on pages 50–51) seems, on the surface, to consist of similar sets – before and after photographs of boys changed by an institution. What's the difference here? Don't be satisfied by saying one set shows an English boy and the other set American Indians, go deeper. And consider the implications of the footnote on page 51. This task would be good to do in class, with discussion.

Finally a rather more complicated sort of difference – three different kinds of source about one subject, Cardinal Beaufort. First comes notes from a biography written in the late nineteenth century.

Second comes an extract from Shakespeare's play *Henry VI* (about three centuries nearer the subject than the biography) and finally an extract from Beaufort's will. Which source do you value most, and why? Put a value (historical of course) on all three sources and give your reasons.

Dotheboys Hall really did exist. Consider these two letters, preserved at the Bowes Museum, and write a short passage on how such educational institutions managed to continue until Dickens' 'investigative journalism' in the form of fiction revealed the truth. You might like to look at *Nicholas Nickleby* to see what was revealed.

1a)

Bowes, Dec '26.ᵗʰ 1818.

Dear Mother,

Christmas here is a time of many pleasures; but the greatest pleasure I feel is that of writing to you. I have only news of an old kind to send you. I am quite well in health, and very happy and hope you and all my relations join me in these blessings. My Master will be in London in a few days upon a three weeks' visit I continue to get on as fast as possible in my learning, and like my school very well. In love to you and all my relations, hoping you may all have a pleasant Christmas and a happy new year;

I am,

Dear Mother,

Your dutiful Son,

John C. Dobson.

1b)

Extract from Henry's Private Letter

Dear Father

Cotherstone Academy
Aug. 7. 1822

Our Master has arrived at Cotherstone
but I was sorry to learn he had no Letter for me
nor any thing else which made me very unhappy, If
you recollect I promised that I would write you a
sly Letter which I assure you I have not forgot and
now an opportunity has come at last & I hope my
dear Father you will not let Mr. Smith know any thing
about it for he would flog me if he knew it and I
hope my dear Father you will write me a Letter as soon
as you receive this but pray dont mention any thing
about this in yours only put a X. at the bottom, Cor
write to my good Friend Mr. Halmer who is very kind
to me and he will give it to me when I go to Church
for he lives opposite and I assure you my dear Father
they are the kindest Friends I have in Yorkshire and
I know he will not show it to Mr. Smith for the Letters
I write you are all examined before they leave the School
and I am obliged to write what Mr. Smith tells us and
the Letters you send me are all examined by Mr. Smith
before I see them, so I hope my dear Father you will
mention nothing of this when you write — It is now
two years come October since I left you at Islington, but
I hope my dear Father you will let me come home at Xmas
that we may once more meet again alive if God permit me
to live as long. Our Bread is nearly black it is made of the
worst Barley Meal, and our Beds are stuffed with chaff
and I assure you we are used more like Bears than Christians
and believe me my dear Father I would rather be obliged to
work all my life time than remain here another year

Edwin is quite well but very unhappy

46

Which view of pre-War Russian government carries most conviction? Why would you choose one, rather than the other?

2a) *Trotsky speaks at trial after 1905 Revolution*

'The prosecution invites you, Gentlemen of the Bench,' he said in his peroration, 'to declare that the Soviet of Workers' Delegates armed the workers for a direct struggle against the actually existing 'form of government'. If you ask me to answer that question categorically, my reply will be: Yes! – Yes, I accept this indictment, but I accept it on a certain condition. And I do not know whether the public prosecutor will be willing to admit this condition or whether the Court will be willing to agree to it. I ask, what precisely does the indictment mean when it speaks of a certain 'form of government'? Does it mean that we have in Russia a genuine form of government? The government for a long time now has been retrenching itself against the nation; it has retreated into the camp of its police and military forces, and of the Black Hundreds. What we have at this moment in Russia is not a national power: it is an automatic machine used to slaughter the population. I do not know how to define otherwise the governmental machine that is tormenting the living body of our country. And if you tell me that the pogroms, the murders, the burnings, the rapes – if you tell me that all that has happened at Tver, at Rostov, at Kursk, at Sedlitz – if you tell me that the events that have occurred at Kishinyov, Odessa, Belostok, represent the form of government of the Russian Empire – then I shall be willing to recognise, in agreement with the public prosecutor, that we took up arms in October and November for the purpose of struggling directly against the form of government that exists in this Empire of Russia.'

2b) Chapter VII The Tsar and His People

All ranks and classes of the Russian people are equally dear to the Emperor. He recognises that part that each class plays in and for the State, enters into their needs, and is wholly occupied with their welfare.

The Tsar's attitude towards the nobility, our highest class, has been clearly shown of late years, particularly on the occasion of the Jubilee celebrations in Moscow and Smolensk and on his visit to Chernigov on September 18th, 1911.

At Moscow on September 9th, 1912, the nobles through their chosen marshals presented the Tsar in the Hall of the Nobility with a banner of ancient Russian design, bearing on one side the face of our Saviour, and on the other that of St George, with the inscription: 'To His Imperial Majesty, from the Russian Nobility.'

Samarin, the marshal of the Moscow nobility, made an animated speech on this occasion, to which His Majesty replied: 'It is with deep sentiments of gratitude and emotion that I have received this banner from your hands. It will always serve to recall to me the enduring and permanent bond which exists between the Russian nobility, the highest class in Russia, and their Tsars. I am convinced that the nobility's spirit of loyalty and devotion to their Tsars, and the boundless love which they and the whole nation bear towards our sacred mother-country, will never die. I beg you to express my sincere and warm gratitude to the highest class in Russia.'

The banner was then taken in procession to the Kremlin Palace, the nobles following it with bared heads. . . . His Majesty showed his kind interest in the Zemstvo (local council) and its work by the visit which he paid during the Poltava celebrations in 1909 to the Poltava district Zemstvo, where he inspected the exhibition of peasant industries of the Poltava Government. Still more markedly did he show his interest in and good-will towards the Zemstvo during his visit, at the time of the 1912 celebrations, to the Moscow depot of peasant industries, built by the Zemstvo, where he and his daughters spent two hours in company with those connected with the institution.

The same good-will was shown towards the townspeople during his visit on the same occasion to the Moscow town hall.

But it is to the welfare and moral development of the peasants, the most numerous class in Russia, but the weakest from the economical point of view, that the Tsar devotes his especial care and attention. In this respect our Sovereign is indeed the 'Little Father' of his people, their good father and friend. No measure to improve the lot of the agricultural peasant passes without the liveliest co-operation of the Tsar, who has expressed himself in the following words on different occasions:

'It is my chief preoccupation to discover the needs of the peasants, who are so dear to me.'

'I am specially concerned with the welfare of the peasants.'

'I am earnestly considering the condition of the peasantry and the question of giving them the land they need.'

'Of all the bills introduced by my direction into the Duma I consider the one which deals with the reform of the land tenure of the peasantry to be the most important.'

'I will not forget the peasants: your needs are near to my heart, and I shall always keep them in mind.'

During the Poltava celebrations (of which I shall speak later) the Emperor visited the camp of the peasant delegates and spoke to them

48

with a kindness and simplicity which affected them to tears. The Tsar was specially interested in their dress, which varied with the district: some had blue belts, others red; some had grey caps, others black and so forth. They were delighted to find that the Tsar could easily pick out the district a man belonged to by his dress. When he praised them for continuing to wear the national costume and expressed a wish that they would always do so, they all said that they themselves would never discard it and would enjoin their children to continue the tradition. The Tsar talked genially with them for a long time, and those who had the honour to converse with him silently and piously crossed themselves, and felt happier for the rest of their lives. The Tsar's visit to the camp lasted about two hours, during the whole of which time such silence reigned that every word the Sovereign spoke was audible at a distance, while not a man moved. At the conclusion the Tsar said: 'I thank you for your love and devotion, my brothers. I shall never forget it.' A mighty 'hurrah' rang out in answer. The Tsar then got into his carriage and drove off to visit the monument raised in memory of the Swedes. The people and the delegates ran after the carriage, and their cheers followed him for a long way.

'God be praised', said the elders among them, 'we have seen the Tsar; now death will be easier.'

'We will hang our belts before the ikons,' said others, whose dress had been noticed 'and our grandchildren may see the belts which the Tsar himself noticed and for wearing which he praised us.'

'The Tsar himself spoke to me,' said those who had been honoured by conversing with the Sovereign. And they all proudly repeated to one another the conversation, forgetting no single word or gesture of the Tsar, crossing themselves piously at the memory of his kindness . . .

Chapter X   National Reforms

At the commencement of the present century Providence sent Russia two heavy trials: the unsuccessful war with Japan and the internal disorders which followed just after the war. Russians who sincerely loved their country went through these sad events with poignant grief in their hearts and full of troubled apprehensions for the future. These events are well known to us all, and we will not dwell on them, to avoid re-opening wounds that have not yet quite healed. Thanks to the prayers of the saints that guard the Russian soil, the wrath of God stopped short of destruction, and Russia has again settled down to peace and quiet. We only mention these events to show that they have not hindered Russia's development, and that the far-reaching reforms indicated by the Tsar on his accession to the throne have promptly been realised and continue to be realised . . .

From Major General Elchaninov's *Tsar Nicholas II* (1913)

The pictures below come from quite a well-known advertisement for Dr Barnardo's homes. On the next page you will see two similar pictures, c). Or *are* they all that similar? In what ways would you regard them as different?

3a)

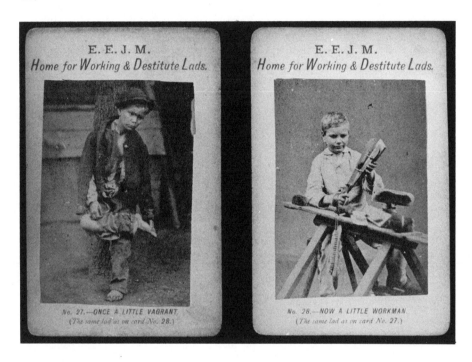

3b)

A group of boys on their arrival at an Indian boarding school in 1878

Some of the same boys fifteen months later

You might like to know that the Dr Barnardo pictures are 'fudged' – both were taken on the same day . . .

There follow:

a) notes from the *Dictionary of National Biography* on the life of Cardinal Beaufort

b) an extract from Shakespeare's *Henry VI*

c) an extract from Beaufort's will.
   Consider which is the most useful source for the political biographer of the Cardinal.

4a) Henry Beaufort was the second illegitimate son of John of Gaunt and Catherine Swynford. His parents later married and he was made legitimate by his cousin the king Richard II. He was educated as a lawyer, and was given rich offices in the Church. In 1398 he was made bishop of Lincoln.

1399 his half brother became king as Henry IV. In 1403 Beaufort was made Chancellor, the most important office in the kingdom; in 1405 he was made Bishop of Winchester, the richest see in the kingdom.

He was very close to the Prince of Wales and when he became king Henry in 1413 he made Beaufort Chancellor again. Beaufort supported the war with France and lent the king huge sums of money to support it. On the king's death he owed Beaufort £20,150.

Beaufort was godfather to the baby king Henry VI and continued to support the king with money. He loaned large sums in return for promises of the customs, with the crown jewels in pledge (all estimated at half their worth).

Beaufort was consistently opposed by Henry V's younger brother, Humphrey Duke of Gloucester. Gloucester was a headstrong war leader, wasting vast sums; Beaufort was the fund-raiser, and well hated for it.

In 1426 Beaufort accepted the cardinal's hat to lead the Papal crusade against the heretic Hussites. In this he showed great courage, nearly turning the retreating army, tearing down their flag and stamping it on the floor to shame them.

Gloucester continued his bitter opposition, trying to remove Beaufort's see of Winchester, and to get him removed from the royal council. In 1433 Beaufort made a bid for the papacy, but despite spending huge sums failed.

He now worked for peace, and struggled hard to achieve it. He died in 1447 shortly after Gloucester. He left £50,000.

He finished Winchester Cathedral, and enlarged St Cross. He left huge sums for masses, and some money to his illegitimate daughter Joan Stradling.

4b) SCENE III. London. Cardinal Beaufort's bedchamber

Enter the King, Salisbury, and Warwick, to the Cardinal in bed.

King	How fares my lord? Speak, Beaufort to thy sovereign.
Cardinal	If thou be'st Death I'll give thee England's treasure, Enough to purchase such another island, So thou wilt let me live and feel no pain.
King	Ah, what a sign it is of evil life Where death's approach is seen so terrible!
Warwick	Beaufort, it is thy sovereign speaks to thee.
Cardinal	Bring me unto my trial when you will Died he not in his bed? Where should he die? Can I make men live, whe'er they will or no? O, torture me no more! I will confess. Alive again? Then show me where he is; I'll give a thousand pound to look upon him. He hath no eyes, the dust hath blinded them. Comb down his hair; look, look! it stands upright, Like lime-twigs set to catch my winged soul! Give me some drink; and bid the apothecary Bring the strong poison that I bought of him.
King	O Thou eternal Mover of the heavens, Look with a gentle eye upon this wretch! O, beat away the busy meddling fiend That lays strong siege upon this wretch's soul, And from his bosom purge this black despair!
Warwick	See how the pangs of death do make him grin.
Salisbury	Disturb him not, let him pass peaceably.
King	Peace to his soul, if God's good pleasure be! Lord Card'nal, if thou think on heaven's bliss, Hold up thy hand, make signal of thy hope. He dies and makes no sign: O God, forgive him!
Warwick	So bad a death argues a monstrous life.
King	Forebear to judge, for we are sinners all. Close up his eyes, and draw the curtain close; And let us all to meditation.

4c) Jewels returned to King

A tablet of gold, called the Tablet of Lancaster, garnished with 16 rubies, three other rubies, 54 pearls and 2 sapphires.

Two basins of gold

One cup of gold covered with filigree work with three scutcheons of the king's arms on top.

One tablet of gold called the Tablet of Burgundy, garnished with 26 rubies, 22 sapphires, 142 pearls.

One image of St George garnished with 8 rubies, 178 pearls.

One tablet of St George garnished with 3 diamonds, 132 rubies, 32 sapphires, 36 rubies, 562 pearls and 3 emeralds.

One image of St Michael garnished with 152 pearls, 4 sapphires, 24 rubies.

Looking at the language of the document

There are five documents in this unit, all built into the theme 'there's more in this than meets the eye'. They all require careful reading, for they may not quite mean what they seem to say, and almost certainly they mean a good deal more.

The first (page 56) is an inscription from a tomb in Sherbourne church. It is an *obituary*, so we should expect that it says only good things about the dead person. But it is in a kind of coded language. Read it first to find out what kind of an impression the writer is trying to give, and record your thoughts on this. Have a second go at it and see whether you can find out what he is really saying – is there a true picture of a real man lurking beneath the language here?

The second piece of text (page 57) is similar to the first, in some ways, a *sampler* woven by a mother for her children, only a little while after friend Hugh Squiers was writing on Education (see page 10). Try to sort out from this text three things:

- the lady's view of the purpose of education;
- her views on youth;
- her attitudes to the roles of the sexes.

Give detailed quotations from the text to show how the language betrays attitudes.

The third (pages 57–60) is a set of extracts from a speech on foreign affairs in the House of Commons in 1587. From the language he uses in the speech, work out Job Throckmorton's assumptions about foreigners and (by implication) about England and the English.

Now look at the next extract (page 60), from a much later date, but still about Englishmen and foreigners. Deduce what the leader

T O18845

writer would really have wanted to say about the Norwegians if he had not been forced to be fair and polite by good manners.

Finally look at the fifth exercise in this unit (page 62). This is rather different in that the two documents presented are secondary rather than primary sources – they are presenting historical explanations of the past. Both are interpreting some past sources – in this case flowers. Look at the explanations the articles provide for these survivals, look particularly at the language they use. Do you find their 'history' convincing? If so, why? If not, again, why? Discuss this one in some detail in class, for in the next unit you will be writing history from documents yourselves, so you had better get ready.

Here lyes John Lord Digby Baron Digby of Sherborne and Earl of Bristol
Titles to which the merit of his grandfather first gave lustre
And which he himself laid down unsully'd
He was naturally enclined to avoid the Hurry of a publick life,
Yet careful to keep up the port of his Quality,
Was willing to be at ease, but scorned obscurity;
And therefore never made his Retirement a pretence to draw
Himself within a narrower compass, or to shun such expence
As Charity, Hospitality, and his Honour call'd for.
His Religion was that which by LAW is Established;
And the conduct of his life shew'd the power of it in his Heart.

His distinction from others never made him forget himself or them:
He was kind & obliging to his Neighbours, generous & condescending to
   his inferiours and just to all Mankind.
Nor had the temptations of honour & pleasure in this world
Strength enough to withdraw his Eyes from that great
Object of his hope, which we reasonably assure ourselves he now enjoys.

He dyed
Sept: xii:
Ann: Dom: MDCICVIII

The following verse is taken from a sampler worked by a lady for her children. Read it with care and attempt to write an account of what values it demonstrates, what the mother hoped her children would gain from their experience of learning:

EDUCATION

Youth like softened Wax with Ease will take
Those images that first impressions make.
If these are fair then actions will be bright
If foul they'll clouded be with shades of night.
Industry laughs in early days
Not only gives the teacher praise
But gives us pleasure when we view
The works that innocence can do
The parents with exulting joy
Survey it as no childish Toy
But as a Prelude that each Day
A greater genius shall display
Go on my dear strive to excell
Improve in work and reading well
For book and needle both contend
To make a Housewife and a Friend

John Lucas   Sarah Lucas

Mary Lucas   May 22 1723   Mary Edward

How far are present day parents' expectations similar to and different from the above?

Job Throckmorton, MP for Warwick, made the following speech in February 1587. It won him a long stretch in the Tower. Why do you think he was so punished and what can the speech tell us about contemporary attitudes?

'we that have lived in the eyes of all men, so choked, as it were, with blessings of God beyond desert, we that have lived to see her Majesty's life, so dear unto us, pulled out, as it were, even out of the lion's jaws in despite of Hell and Satan, may truly – not in any pride of heart, but in humbleness of soul to our comforts – confess that indeed the Lord hath vowed himself to be English . . . It is an argument unanswerable, to prove the Pope to be that man described in the Apocalypse – I mean that man of sin, that beast with the mark in his forehead – to prove him, I say, to be Antichrist . . . that look! where he curseth the Lord continually blesseth, and on the contrary, where he blesseth the finger of God's wrath is never from thence. Mark it, I pray you, well.'

'For France, Catherine de Medici (I hope I need not describe her) hath not many (thanks be to God) left of her loins to pester the earth with. And those that she hath yet living, truly – to speak indifferently – she may have as much comfort of them as the adder hath of her brood. Whether they sucked their mother's breast, I know not; but sure, if they did not, it seemeth their nurses were greatly to blame, instead of milk to suckle them up with blood from their infancy . . . Queen Mother may . . . brag above all women in Europe, that she hath brought us into this world such a litter (to her praise be it spoken) as few women have done . . .; whose principal delight . . . hath been in nothing almost but in hypocrisy, filthiness of life, and persecuting of the church of God. As to him that now holdeth the sceptre there [Henry III], do ye not see him smitten [with] barrenness? Is that all? Nay, do ye not see him stricken with a fearful kind of giddiness, as it were a man in a trance or ecstasy', drawn sometimes to the Guisan faction, sometimes underhand to the King of Navarre? It may truly be said of him, 'He is afraid of shadows that feareth not the Lord'.

Philip II was next anatomized: his profession superstitious, 'his religion idolatrous, his life some think licentious, his marriage we all know incestuous, great-uncle to his own children'. Can there come any greater plague to a Prince than this – to leave his dominions 'to be possessed by an incestuous race of bastards'; to sit down in his chair in his old age 'and behold the ruin of his house before his face'? He possesses 'many rich countries, populous nations, golden mines, and I know not what'. Mighty as he is, 'the Lord hath put a snaffle in his mouth for all that'. His dominions are rather a burden than a defence; his receipts do little more than answer his disbursements; 'maugre his head', he is forced to make peace with the sworn enemy of all Christendom. 'Have we not lived to see him stricken with a sottish kind of madness', yielding 'to the drawing of the heart blood of his own son', and suffering 'his wife to be in the house of [the] Inquisition?'

'A man with half an eye may easily behold the judgment of God upon both these kings, notwithstanding the blessing of the Holy Father. Whether any of them hath the leprosy of the body, I know not; but we are well assured both of them have the lethargy of the soul – that is, the sleeping sickness'.

Throckmorton warned Members against a sense of security, bred by the rare and blessed peace they had enjoyed under her Majesty's government – a government 'in wisdom equal, in mildness and mercy superior' to that of all her progenitors. Coming to his principal point, which was to urge acceptance of the sovereignty of the Netherlands, he described this offer as 'an evident sign that the Lord hath yet once more vowed himself to be English, notwithstanding all our former unthankfulness and wretched deserts'. He pictured God addressing them from Heaven: 'Though your sins do swarm in abundance . . . if ye will reform your church and lives in time, I will here offer you a means whereby ye shall be able to stand alone, yea, and to withstand all the foreign invasions of your ungodly enemies'.

If we neglect this offer of the Low Countries, where else, he asked, is there any other anchor-hold of safety? 'Our dear brother of France . . . howsoever we league it or temporize it with him', is in far deeper league with our sworn and professed enemy, Spain. 'In whom there is no religion, in him there is no trust. A Frenchman unreformed is as vile a man as lives, and no villainy can make him blush.'

'Whither, then, shall we cast our eye?' he asked. 'Northward towards the young imp of Scotland? Alas! it is a cold coast (ye know) and he that should set up his rest upon so young and wavering a head might happen find cold comfort . . . Ye knew his mother, I am sure: did ye not? Then I hope ye will all join with me in this prayer: that whatsoever his father was, I beseech the Lord he take not after his mother . . . How he may degenerate from the humour of his ancestors, I know not.' As a boy, I heard it said that falsehood was the very nature of a Scot. It may be that religion and good education have saved him from corruption: we hope they have. But her Majesty should keep a jealous and watchful eye on him. The Catholic leader, Dr. Allen, has commended him. 'When a man of Allen's humour falls a-praising of him . . . can he be an ill-minded subject amongst us that thereupon . . . feareth some mischief?'

Throckmorton continued: 'We see no hope of Spain, no trust in France, cold comfort in Scotland. Whither then shall we direct our course?' The very finger of God directs us to the Low Countries, as though to say: 'There only is the means of your safety, there only is the passage laid open unto you, there only, and nowhere else, is the vent of your commodities.' The action is lawful. These countries never were an 'absolute government'. The King of Spain has lost the right of his sovereignty 'by tyranny and blood, or rather, if ye will, by the just judgment of God.' Throckmorton was sure that the people there 'desire, even from the bottom of their hearts, to live under the obeissance of her Majesty, before any other prince or potentate of the earth', having tasted 'the sweetness and equality of her Majesty's government under an honourable general [the Earl of Leicester], who, by his wisdom, hath emblazoned her name there and renowned her sceptre to posterity'. The Queen's purpose had been 'to succour the afflicted for the cause of religion'. The Romans, for their own glory, had written 'in their ensigns', *parcere subiectis et debellare superbos*: may the Lord, not for her glory but for His, vouchsafe that Elizabeth in her ensigns write, *sceptrum afflictae ecclesiae consecratum* – my sceptre dedicated to the afflicted Church.

To those who might object that this policy would 'pull Spain on our heads', he answered: Better that, than 'pull the wrath of God on our heads'. As Elisha was saved from the Syrian army by the host of Heaven, so might they be. It was not Spain nor France they had to fear, but the lack of true Christian discipline. 'Our bodies are in England, our hearts are at Rome.' Mere outward conformity is what our spiritual governors seem to desire and our carnal gospellers to practise. If it would please the Lord so to work on her Majesty's heart that this was reformed, 'then should we not need to fear either the fury of Spain, or the treachery of France, or the hosts of the Assyrians, or all the power of Hell and darkness.'

Sir John Neal, *Elizabeth and her Parliaments, 1581–1601*
(1957) pt ii, cap iv

The South Pole Won

MARCH 9, 1912

The leader writer's hope that it was possible Scott 'reached the Pole before December 14' was not realized. Captain Scott (1868–1912) with Dr E. A. Wilson, Capt L. E. G. ('Titus') Oates, Lt H. R. Bowers and P/O E. Evans reached the South Pole on January 18, 1912. They perished in appalling weather on the return journey; Scott's last entry in his diary was on March 29; the tent containing the bodies of Scott, Wilson and Bowers was found on November 12, 1912.

It is clear from the tidings sent by CAPTAIN AMUNDSEN that he reached the South Pole in the middle of December, and thus secured the last great trophy of Polar exploration. The whole British nation will offer its congratulations to CAPTAIN AMUNDSEN and the Norwegians on this dashing achievement. There is no need to pretend that we should not have been glad to see the most conspicuous triumph in Antarctic exploration secured by the British expedition bound, among other objects, on the same quest. But we may be sure that wherever CAPTAIN SCOTT may be, or whatever point he may have reached in the Antarctic midsummer, he would be the first to acclaim the success of that truly hardy Norseman, who has already realized the oldest and most romantic dream of Arctic exploration by his navigation of the North-West Passage. If Englishmen were not

to attain the chief goal of exploration at either of the earth's extremities, there are no nations to whom they would more gladly see the prizes fall than to their kinsmen of the United States and of Norway.

It is to be understood from CAPTAIN AMUNDSEN's message that he reached the South Pole on December 14, and remained there until the 17th, for the purpose of taking the noon observation for several consecutive days, and thus of veryifying his position beyond any shadow of doubt. We have still to hear the story of CAPTAIN SCOTT's expedition during the Antarctic summer; and it is by no means unlikely that he also succeeded in his chief endeavour, and, indeed, possible that he reached the Pole before December 14. The Pole is not as concrete or localized an object as the posts which mark the end of a given distance on a running track; and the flag or other signal of victory which one explorer set up to show that he had got there might easily be blown down and covered by snow, or hidden by bad weather from the next visitor to the same rather indeterminate spot. It is at present useless to discuss these varied possibilities; we must simply 'wait and see.' The success of CAPTAIN SCOTT would undoubtedly be received in this country with all the more gratification from the fact that his expedition did not aim solely at reaching the Pole, but was systematically equipped for carrying our many branches of scientific investigation which should ultimately prove of much greater value to humanity. It will be remembered that the announcement of CAPTAIN AMUNDSEN'S intention to attack the South Pole was received last spring with considerable surprise, as he had for some time been collecting funds for an expedition into North Polar regions, and gave an address explaining this object before the Royal Geographical Society in January, 1909. Although his change of plan must have necessitated several months' preparations, it was not announced even to his own crew, and it was not until his vessel reached Madeira that his determination was announced to sail South instead of North. The first authentic news of his presence in Antarctic regions came from CAPTAIN SCOTT who found the Fram in the Bay of Whales in February last year, preparing to leave CAPTAIN AMUNDSEN in winter quarters. This sudden change of plan and the unnecessary secrecy which surrounded it were felt to be not quite in accordance with the spirit of fair and open competition which had hitherto marked Antarctic exploration. The enterprise appeared in the light of a mere dash for the Pole, designed to forestall the British expedition in the most spectacular, though not the most valuable, part of its work; and although British feeling would have been fully in sympathy with such an enterprise if openly declared, circumstances of its inception produced a less favourable impression. We may sincerely congratulate CAPTAIN AMUNDSEN on the skill and daring with which he had carried out his plans, and added a great triumph to a fine record. But our national sympathy and admiration will none the less be accorded to CAPTAIN SCOTT and his comrades of the British expedition if they have lost the credit of reaching the South Pole first, or even if they do not reach it.

The Times

61

Read the following two cuttings (they both come from *The Times*, the first 12.11.75, the second 13.2.76). The explanations offered in both tend to suggest that men throughout time have had a certain attitude to flowers, and the writers are aware of the romantic implications of these findings. Could there be other, more prosaic explantions? Would you prefer these? What significance might we attach to these findings?

Science report

Mortality: Floral burial

The custom of placing flowers on the graves of the dead goes back to the very beginnings of civilization and can provide archaeologists with a means of bringing the past vividly to life. Modern techniques of pollen analysis have now shown that one day in early summer more than 50,000 years ago, a Neanderthal man discovered by archaeologists 15 years ago in the Zagros mountains of Iraq, and named Shanidar IV, was laid in his grave on a bed of brilliantly coloured wild flowers.

Arlette Leroi-Gourham of the Musée de l'Homme in Paris, has anlaysed the pollen found in the Shanidar IV grave and describes in a recent issue of *Science* how the grave may have been arranged. Large clusters of pollen of various types of flowers were found, in the soil under the skeleton, some still in the form of the anther, showing that the pollen had not simply blown in from the outside.

The most abundant pollen came from flowers of the *Senecio* family – the rag-worts which have bright golden yellow flowers, and from *Achillea*, which contains yellow and creamy white flower species. Pollen from the yellow St

Barnaby's thistle was also indentified, as well as several clusters of the brilliant blue *Muscari*, wild relatives of the garden grape hyacinth. Mixed in with them were clusters of pollen from *Ephedra*, whose flexible, highly branched stems lend themselves well to the construction of bedding on which the dead could have been laid.

In one of the samples a scale from a butterfly's wing was found among the pollen and, as the author remarks, it needs little imagination to suppose that a butterfly had alighted on one of the flowers and was later brought into the cave.

Nowadays, in the Zagros mountains, the flowers found in the cave bloom during May and June, so, even allowing for a slight shift in the flowering period as a result of a change in the climate from the more humid conditions then obtaining, Shanidar IV was un-doubtedly laid in his grave sometime between the end of May and early July.

By Nature-Times News Service
Source: *Science* 190 (November 7) 562; 1975.
© **Nature-Times News Service, 1975.**

Romsey Abbey workmen discover rose with petals intact after 850 years

By Philip Howard

Workmen have discovered what seems to be the oldest botanical specimen ever found in Europe in the east wall of Romsey Abbey. It is a rose, hidden in the wall more than eight and a half centuries ago.

The oldest rose in the world was discovered romantically two days before St Valentine's day, by workmen removing medieval paintings from the east wall. They noticed that the putlog holes, used by workmen in the Middle Ages to support scaffolding, had been uncharacteristically plastered over.

They removed the plaster and found the rose, about an inch and a half in diameter, with a twig and numerous petals and leaves. It is wizened and sere, very fragile, but perfectly preserved.

Yesterday Dr Jane Renfrew, a paleobotanist, spent four hours removing it with infinitesimal delicacy, and it was taken to London for conservation treatment at the Natural History Museum.

Mr Kevin Stubbs, director of archaeology for the Test Valley, says that the rose can be dated precisely. The *terminus ante quem* is 1270, when the wall paintings were made over the undisturbed putlog holes.

Mr Stubbs says: 'However, there was no reason for the putlog holes to be opened in 1270, and we believe that they have been sealed since the completion of the east wall in 1120. The placing of the rose might have been a romantic gesture by one of the masons who built the abbey.'

The roses of Romsey are inveterately famous. One of the earliest historical references to a formal flower garden in Britain concerns a visit by William Rufus to Romsey Abbey in 1093.

It says: 'The King entered the cloister as if to inspect the roses and other flowers.' The Romsey rose is young compared with the oldest botanical specimen yet found, a posy recovered from Tutankhamun's tomb. But it is still an extremely important event for paleobotany.

Different conservation treatments are to be tried to discover the most suitable. It may even be possible to revive the seeds so that the old rose blooms again. After its treatment at the Natural History Museum, it will be examined by Dr Melville of the Royal Botanic Gardens at Kew.

Writing history from the sources

In fact you have been doing this right from the start of your work. Each time you analyse a document, select pieces from it, rearrange its information, express an opinion about it or suggest an explanation for it, you are doing history. But now we will do it selfconsciously.

We will take three steps:

- in the first section we shall use documents to illustrate or illuminate the past;

- in the second section we will attempt to write a story out of sources;

- in the third section we will go the whole hog.

Illustrating the past with source materials

In this section I am just asking you to provide an historical commentary for each document or group of sources. Say what it reminds you of, what it makes you think, whether it proves a point, whether you could develop an argument about the past from it.

The documents are:

1   a) An extract from a board of guardians' minute book and b) a bread ticket

2   a) A photograph of the servants at Cliveden, 1910, and b) a report of the will of the Earl of Warwick, 1984

3a) and b) Two pictures illustrating the collapse of the mark in Germany in 1922

4a) and b) Extracts from a guidebook to Europe of 1938.

In preparing your commentary on these documents don't hesitate to use the library to look up background details. For example, you might need to know quite a bit more about Mussolini's Italy before you feel ready to comment on **4**. Go ahead – help yourself – it is excellent practice.

This document is an entry from the Minute Book of the Bromsgrove Board of Guardians for 20 April, 1840. The Guardians are putting into action the principles of 'less eligibility' in the new Poor Law. In what ways might we criticise their action? Would our criticism be fair?

1a) The Clerk read a circular issued by the Poor Law Commissioners dated the 18th March last, which has been received by the Auditor, instructing him to disallow in the accounts any expenditure which shall henceforth be incurred in the extra allowances supplied to the Inmates of the Workhouse on Christmas day and other festive occasions. The Commissioners conceiving it to be unjust to apply the proceeds of a compulsory tax raised only to relieve destitution to provide for the Inmates of a Workhouse luxuries which are beyond the reach of many of those by whom the tax is paid.

Worcester County Record Office BA400 251

Write a detailed historical commentary on what was happening when the ticket given below was used:

1b)

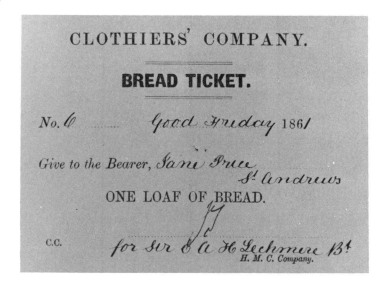

What commentary would you supply for picture **2a)**, showing the servants of one family? What sort of judgement might you make about the family? How fair do you think your judgement would be? What affects the way we think about such things from the past?

Now look at cutting **2b)**. How have things changed in 74 years?

2a)

2b)

Latest wills
Earl of Warwick leaves £69

Earl of Warwick, of Geneva, Switzerland, who during his lifetime passed his estates in Britain, including Warwick Castle, to his family to avoid death duties, left estate in England and Wales valued at £69 net.

The Times 24.10.84

In 1922 the German mark was valued at 1810 to the pound. In 1914 the exchange rate had been 20.43 to £1. Below is a picture of a hundred thousand mark note, and a photograph of a German shopkeeper – who had to use a teachest to hold his takings, since the wads of almost value-less banknotes would not fit into the till.

How is it possible to live with a collapsed currency? Can a nation recover? How does this explain the course of German history in the second quarter of our century? How do such things happen? Could they happen to us?

3a)

A hundred thousand mark banknote at the time of the inflation in Germany after the 1914–18 War.

3b)

GERMAN INFLATION 1922
New pictures from Berlin. Once upon a time the cash register was too big. Now they need big tea chests if they are to get all the money in.

In 1938 Aldor's published their usual holiday guide to Europe. Two extracts are given below. How might one use these in considering the policy of appeasement of the British Government in relation to Fascist governments in Europe at that time?

4a)

1938 IN EUROPE

SPAIN

OWING to the tragic civil war which is still proceeding in Spain, we are omitting the guide to that country from the present issue. It is our fervent hope that we shall be in a position to re-insert it into our 1939 edition.

THE EDITOR

4b)

V – A FEW DONT'S

In deciding to travel to Italy you are probably prompted by a desire to visit a new world. Do not, therefore, be surprised if on crossing the frontier into Italy you encounter people and customs that seem strange to you and may not be pleasant at first. But, then, had you wanted to enjoy your usual environment you would have stayed at home. The general code of behaviour is practically the same all over the civilised world, with a few local variations. In Italy, as everywhere else, there are pleasant and unpleasant, courteous and discourteous people. Generally speaking, the Italian is very courteous and always pleased to assist the foreign visitor. If you encounter the exception to this rule, ask yourself, with your hand on your heart, whether your own country is entirely peopled by angels.

No Politics, Please!

It may easily happen that as you cross the frontier you will find yourself in a crowd of Italian travellers, and you are therefore advised not to talk politics. If your fellow travellers broach the subject, tell them that you are neither an Ambassador nor a Minister of Foreign Affairs, and that you are more interested in Fra Angelico or Leonardo da Vinci than in politics. Naturally, it is not my intention to influence you to suppress your views, nor does anyone in Italy demand this. But politics are a delicate subject and I am sure you do not wish to get into difficulties on account of a misinterpreted remark. So leave politics alone. If you wish to enjoy your stay in Italy to the full, do not be too critical.

Writing stories from sources

Some people pretend to despise narrative, laughing at historians who try to write history 'as it actually happened' in terms of a sequence of events. Of course simple story telling over-simplifies the picture (and often suggests that individuals and events had a much greater role than was in fact the case), and of course we can never *really* know. But, that said, *all* historians are always spinning narrative out of sources – they can't escape it, it is how history always works.

I am asking two simple questions about the sources in this section:

1 From the documents in the first collection can you prepare a satisfactory story that you believe is as close to the truth as possible, about the English capture of the foreign shipping? Beware, these documents contradict each other like fury – this is the hardest exercise you have yet had.

2 From the documents in the second collection, can you prepare a detailed and accurate account of the events leading up to the murder of Admiral Coligny and his actual death? This one isn't easy, either! But it will get you quite close to writing history, for generations of historians have tried to explain how the massacre of St Bartholomew's day came to happen.

The following letters are taken from the *Fugger Archives*. The Fuggers were a multinational trading company who needed lots of information. Try to turn them into a true story.

Middleburg, October 9 1592

The English have brought the great Indian ship Santa Maria into Portsmouth. The warships have stolen half her cargo and have tried hard to sell the spices in all quarters, though they are forbidden to do so. But forbidding is no use, for Her Majesty and others cannot reduce the sailors to obedience. Most of the valuables on this ship will be lost. There were no pearls on board. They brought no Portugese to England, so as to be able to pillage easier. They also burnt all bills of lading and ship's papers. Pepper, cinnamon, cloves and indigo form the bulk of cargo, but especially pepper, 8000 cwt. The English warships are mostly at home. They have taken another three ships which defended themselves. These were also pillaged.

In England the plague is still raging. The Court and others of importance have left London for the country.

Antwerp, October, 10 1592

The Portugese here have letters from London of the 26th ult. informing them that the Captain's ship from Calicut has been brought to London and that cloves to the value of £6000 have already been sold off her. But the Queen has caused the sale of merchandise from this ship to be suspended in order that she may settle the price at which goods are to be sold, so as to obtain a higher rate. What arrangements have been made about the other two ships from Calicut is unknown.

Antwerp, October 11, 1592

Letters of the 9th inst. from Middelburg report that the English have again brought in 4 ships to England, one of which from Brazil is laden with sugar, one from St Thomas with hides, and the other two, bound for the Spanish mines, with 1600 barrels of quicksilver. All this is valued at over 60,000 crowns. At Middleburg are 27 companies of English soldiers, waiting for the first favourable wind to sail to Brittany.

The English are said to have brought a Calicut ship into Portsmouth and to have taken off her some 200 barrels. In these barrels were quantities of pearls and jewels, and gold in bullion. They have also got a large amount of spices, such as 4500 cwt. of pepper, cinnamon, nutmegs, mace and cloves. This alone would amount to over £200,000. The English have fought a good deal over the loot.

London letters of the 2nd inst. state that the Calicut ship brought into Portsmouth by the English is named the Madre de Dios and is of 1500 tons with 36 brass guns. There were 90 sailors and numerous passengers on board. The value was far above a million, as the spices among the cargo had been valued at a million, and there were also on board gold costumes, a lot of Calicut linen and much Chinese silk. At first she fought with two English ships only, but when nine English ships with Lord Cumberland came up the Calicut ship had to surrender. Two hundred lives are said to have been lost on each side. The lesser people were put ashore on the island of Flores, and only sixteen of the most important were brought to England. The other ship which was burnt off the Azores was named the Santa Cruz.

(The great ship Madre de Dios was taken by Sir John Burgh, 1562–1593. Flores is one of the Azores.)

Antwerp, October 13, 1592

London letters of the 10th inst. report that the Queen has given strict orders on pain of severe punishment for the return of all property off the Calicut ship brought into England. What has already been sold must be reported at Court and paid for. It is hoped that by this means the jewels and other valuables will reappear. It is thought also that the price of pepper will not come down, especially as the pepper on the Santa Cruz was lost.

Middleburg, November 18, 1592

Our only news here is that the two East Indian caravels taken by the English have been brought into Plymouth. Their value is estimated at above £20,000. The Viceroy with his whole family and all his fortune is on board. Ships still at sea are in utmost danger, so that numerous Portugese must be ruined, for far too many of their Brazilian ships have been taken. Very much pepper seems to have been on board and this will not suit the traders, as they already have 6000 cwt. stored in Amsterdam.

Middleburg, November 19, 1592

Letters from London of the 17th inst. confirm that two ships from Spain to Peru with quicksilver have been taken by the English. It is said that the losses of the King of Spain at sea this year could not be paid for with four millions.

The death of Admiral Coligny

Gaspard de Coligny, Admiral of France had been very much in charge of the aspirations of Charles IX from 12 September 1571. As leader of the French Protestants, he aimed at an English alliance, a marriage between the King's sister and Henry of Navarre, and a joint attack on Spain in the Low Countries. The King's mother, Catherine de Medici, had been the leading power in France since the death of her husband in July 1559. She aimed at a balanced policy, and was above all terrified of war with Spain. In April 1572 the English alliance was made. In May detachments of French Protestants invaded the Low Countries. On 7 July Henry of Navarre arrived in Paris for the wedding. The wedding took place 18 August. Catherine had planned with the Guises (leaders of the Catholic party) to assassinate Coligny, no doubt secretly hoping that Coligny's friends would take revenge and assassinate the Guises. The attempt on Coligny's life failed on August 22nd (the assassin missing because he bent to tie up his shoe laces). The King was still in favour of Coligny, calling him as ever, 'mon père'. Catherine persuaded the King that the Huguenots would take a massive revenge, and so reduced him that he ordered all to be killed. At four o'clock in the morning the massacre commenced at Coligny's house. The King took an enthusiastic part, shooting from the balcony of the Louvre. Two to three thousand were killed in Paris, possibly ten thousand in the provinces.

That which Juan de Olaegui, secretary to the ambassador Don Diego de Çuniga, coming from the court of France with the ambassador's dispatches for Your Majesty, relates concerning the occurrences that have happened at that court.
On Thursday, 27th August, at eleven in the morning, the Admiral, having left the palace, stopped to read a letter that a Huguenot gentleman had just given him, at some fifty or sixty paces from the palace. From a neighbouring house he was hit by an arquebus shot, which carried away one finger of his right hand and went through his arm and left hand; the ball came out near his elbow: when he felt the wound he said nothing but that they should find out who had done it.

The man who had fired the shot got out by a back door in the said house; he mounted a horse that was held ready for him; he left Paris by a gate where there was a Spanish horse awaiting him, and two leagues farther on he found another, a Turkish horse.

About four hundred mounted men, all Huguenots, set off in pursuit of the man who had wounded the Admiral, but they could not catch up with him and they came back to Paris that same day, the 22nd; that day and the next, it was widely said among the Huguenots that the Most Christian King or the Duke of Anjou were not strangers to this attempt; they further said that it had been committed by order of the dukes of Guise and Aumale, or of the Duke of Alba, and they threatened heaven and earth with unspeakable boldness and insolence.

The same day, 22nd August, the Most Christian King and his mother went to visit the Admiral, who said to the king that even if he were to lose his left arm, he would still have his right with which to avenge himself for the offence that had been done to him, and two hundred thousand men to help him; to which the king replied that although he was the ruler he had not been able to assemble fifty thousand and could not now.

After this visit, the king having returned to the palace, the Prince of Condé came to him and required him to take some measures about what had just happened; for if he did not, he was well able to revenge himself. The king satisfied him, but nevertheless as the said prince has a fiendish mind he continued threatening the king and people.

On the said day, the king retired to his apartments early and went to bed at eight or nine o'clock. At ten he got up and summoned Marcel, the head of the citizens of Paris; he bade him tell certain captains of the townsmen to hold themselves ready with their companies until they should hear the ringing of the alarm. Marcel carried out this command.

At midnight on 23rd August the king sent for the dukes of Montpensier, Guise and Aumale, together with the Bastard of Angoulême: he told each what it was that he had to do, which was that the Duke of Montpensier should search the apartments of the princes of Béarn and Condé to see who was there, and that then the guard should kill such and such, whom he named; that the dukes of Guise and Aumale, with the bastard, should

72

cut off the head of the Admiral and those of his suite and that they should try to take and to kill Montgomery and the Vidame of Chartres, who were staying in the Faubourg Saint-Germain, outside the gates: they took measures to this effect, but without success, for these men escaped and fled into Normandy.

On Sunday, Saint Bartholomew's day, at three o'clock in the morning, the alarm was rung: all the Parisians began killing the Huguenots of the town, breaking down the doors of the houses in which they lived and pillaging what they found within.

The said Guise, Aumale and Angoulême went to the Admiral's house, which they entered, having killed eight of the Prince of Béarn's Swiss who tried to defend it.

They went up to his room, and in the bed in which he was lying, the Duke of Guise shot him in the head with a pistol; then they took him and threw him naked out of the window into the courtyard of his house, where he received several more strokes with swords and daggers.

When they tried to throw him out of the window he said, 'Oh, Monsieur, have pity on old age', but he was not given time to say any more.

This slaughter took place in sight of the king, who watched it with great pleasure. A few days later, he went himself to see the gibbet at Montfaucon where Coligny's body was hanging by the feet, and as some of his train affected not to go near because the body stank, 'The smell of a dead enemy,' said he, 'is sweet and delightful.'

(*Histoire de Charles IX*, by Papyre Masson, *historiographer to the king*.)

THE OREMUS AFTER THE THANKSGIVING MASS CELEBRATED AT THE CHURCH OF SAINT-LOUIS-DES-FRANÇAIS IN ROME 'FOR THE VERY GREAT BLESSING RECEIVED FROM GOD'.

Almighty God, Who rejecteth the proud and blesseth the humble, we offer Thee the tribute of our most fervent praise, because taking heed of Thy servants' faith, Thou hast granted them a splendid triumph over the treacherous enemies of the Catholic people; and we humbly beg Thee in Thy mercy to continue what Thou hast in Thy faithfulness begun, for the glory of Thy name, upon which we call. May this be granted, in the name of Christ.

THE ACCOUNT OF FILIPPO CAVRIANA, A MANTUAN PHYSICIAN IN THE SERVICE OF CATHERINE DE' MEDICI.

All night long there was a council at the Louvre. The guards were doubled, and so that the Admiral's suspicions should not be aroused, no one was allowed to leave without showing the king's express order. All the ladies were gathered in the queen's room, and being ignorant of what was being prepared, they were half dead with fear. In the end, when it came to the point of execution, the queen told them that traitors had determined to kill her on the coming Tuesday, her, the king and the whole court, all of which was proved by letters that she had received. At this news the ladies were struck with amazement. The king did not undress, but, laughing, he took the opinions of those who made up the council, such as Guise, Nevers, Montpensier, Tavannes, Retz, Birague and Morvillier. When Morvillier, whom they had woken up, and who had come much disturbed at having been sent for by the king at such a time, learned from His Majesty's mouth the subject of this nocturnal council, he felt his heart seized with such a terror that before the king had even asked his opinion he collapsed in his seat, incapable of uttering a single word. When he was a little better, his Majesty asked him to state his views. 'Sire,' he replied, 'it is a very serious affair, and one of the highest importance, which might cause the civil war to break out again, more implacable than ever.' Then, as the king pressed him and showed him the imminent peril, he ended after much hesitation and many devious turns by concluding that if all he was told was true, the will of the king and the queen would have to be done and the Huguenots put to death. And as he spoke he could not keep back his sighs and his tears.

Without waiting any longer, the king sent for the King of Navarre and the Prince of Condé; and at this extraordinary hour they came to the king's chamber, accompanied by the men of their train. When these wished to come in – and among them were Monin and Piles – they were stopped at the door by the soldiers of the guard. Then the King of Navarre, turning towards his people with a sorrowful face, said to them, 'Adieu, my friends: God knows whether I shall see you again.'

At the same moment Guise left the palace and went to find the captain of the citizens to give him the order to arm two thousand of his men and to surround the Faubourg Saint-Germain, where more than fifteen hundred Huguenots were living, so that the massacre might take place on both banks of the river at the same time.

Nevers, Montpensier and the other lords at once armed themselves, and together with their people, some on foot, some mounted, went to the various posts that had been allotted to them, all prepared to act in concert.

The king and his brothers did not leave the Louvre.

Cossein, the Gascon commander, the German Besme, a former page to Monsieur de Guise, Hautefort, the Italians Pierre Paul Tossinghi and Petrucci, went with a numerous troop to the house of the Admiral, whom they had orders to kill. They broke down the door and went up the stairs. At the top of it they found a kind of makeshift barricade, made of chests and benches hurriedly heaped together. They thrust their way into the room, found eight or ten servants, whom they killed, and saw the Admiral, standing at the foot of his bed and dressed in a furred gown. The day was only just dawning and things could barely be made out. They asked him, 'Are you the Admiral?' He replied that he was. They rushed at him and covered him with insults. Besme grasped his sword and made to plunge it into his bosom. But he cried out, 'Ah, young soldier, have pity upon old age!' Vain words. With one stroke Besme laid him at his feet: they fired two pistols straight into his face and left him lying there lifeless. The whole house was given over to pillage. Meanwhile some of these men appeared on the balcony and said, 'He is dead.' Those below, Guise and the others, would not believe it. They asked him to be thrown out of the window, which was done. The corpse was stripped, and when it was naked pieces were cut off it . . .

. . . It is said the Coligny, talking to his son-in-law Téligny a week ago about the prediction of an astrologer who had said that he would be hanged, made game of it and said, 'Consider whether there is any likelihood of such a thing happening – unless indeed it means that I shall be hanged in effigy, as I was some months ago.' Now the astrologer had told the truth, for his body, dragged about the streets and the object of the vilest insults, was beheaded and hanged by the feet from the gibbet of Montfaucon, there to become meat for crows.

Such was the miserable end of the man who not long before was the master of half France. Upon him there was found a medal with these words engraved, *Either a complete victory, or an assured peace, or an honourable death.* None of these wishes was to come true.

A TRIBUTE TO CATHERINE DE' MEDICI FROM THE AMBASSADOR OF VENICE.
As there are different views upon this matter of the Huguenots and the Admiral's death, and as people wonder whether it was all an accident or whether it was a premeditated plan, I think it my duty to let your Serenity know what I have learned of the matter from highly-placed persons who are admitted to the secrets of this kingdom. Your Serenity is to know, therefore, that this entire business, from beginning to end, has been the work of the queen, a work conceived, worked out and brought to a conclusion by her, with the help only of the Duke of Anjou, her son. The queen certainly had it in mind for a long while, since lately she herself asked Monsignor Salviati, a relation, who is Nuncio in France, to remember and bear witness of what she had secretly charged him to tell the late Pope, to wit, that he would presently see the vengeance that she and the king would take upon those of the [Protestant] religion. It was with no other end in view that she worked so zealously for the marriage of her daughter with Navarre, without heeding either the King of Portugal or the other great matches that were offered her; and all this to cause the marriage to be held in Paris in the presence of the Admiral and the other leaders of the party, as she supposed the thing would happen and because there was no other way nor a better opportunity for drawing them thither.

On 22nd August, 1572, the Admiral, going from the Louvre in Paris towards his house to dine, was reading a letter, and as he passed before the house of a canon who had formerly been the tutor of the Lord of Guise, an arquebus charged with four balls was fired at him, whereby the finger next to his thumb on his right hand was shot off and his left hand shot in the palm; the ball, passing along the arm and breaking all his bones, came out two fingers above the elbow. The front door of this house was locked and the back open, where there was a Spanish horse upon which he who had wounded the Admiral fled. When the Admiral felt himself wounded, with his Huguenots he took counsel to kill the king and Messieurs his brothers and the queen, saying that this evil came about through them; he decided forthwith to go to his four hundred men who were in the Faubourg Saint-Germain, a thing that would have been easy to do at any time that he wished; but he could not do it so secretly that the king and the queen would not know: for the Admiral having sent for the King of Navarre to the place where he lay, he said these words, or words to this effect, 'My lord, I believe that you know how much I served my lord your father and my late lord your uncle, the Prince of Condé; and as I wish to continue in the same good will towards you and as I am now mortally wounded (for the balls were poisoned) I have decided to make my will before dying and to leave you the realm of France as an inheritance.' And he made known to him the means that he had prepared.

The King of Navarre, having heard all this, returned to his apartments (in the Louvre) and there, very sad and melancholy, foreseeing the great disaster to his brother the king and others, he was so much importuned by his wife that he straightway told her what the said Admiral had decided; and when she understood this, after admonishing him several times not to sully his hands with the blood of the king his brother-in-law, she at once went to tell the king and the queen her mother.

Thus, on Saint Bartholomew's day, the 24th of the said month, at one in the morning, there entered into the said Admiral's house the dukes of Guise and Aumale, and the Chevalier d'Angoulême; and some of their suite entered into the aforesaid Admiral's room, which the Admiral's people defended with their swords; but they were at once defeated. Seeing this, the Admiral went back into his bed and feigned death, but he was drawn out of it by his wounded arm. As Monsieur Cousin set himself to throw him out of the window he put his foot against the wall, for which reason the aforesaid Cousin said to him, 'What, you cunning fox, do you thus feign death?' With these words he threw him down into the courtyard of the house, where the duke of Guise was waiting, to whom he said, 'There, my lord, there is the traitor who was the cause of your father's death.' The aforesaid Guise having heard this, he came to the admiral and said these words to him, 'So there you are, you evil man: God grant, in sooth, but that I do not soil my hands with your blood,' and giving him a kick he went from him. Then directly some person came and shot him in the head with a pistol. This done, they began to drag him on a hurdle through the town. A gentleman cut off his head with a knife, and putting it on the end of his sword he carried it through the town crying, 'Here is the head of the evil man who did so many wrongs to the realm of France!' And as the people belonging to the parliament strove to have the body of the said Admiral back again to carry out the first sentence pronounced against him during the troubles, it was so much dismembered that none of it has been able to be recovered. If they had waited four hours before performing this, the Admiral would have done to them what the said princes have done to him, and would have killed the king and Messieurs his brothers . . .

A PARISIAN CURÉ'S ACCOUNT OF THE MURDER OF COLIGNY.

On Saturday, between ten and eleven o'clock in the evening, the king having heard that the Huguenots were planning to cut his throat, kill his brothers and sack the city of Paris, the Louvre was shut up and he determined to put his enemies to death. He then sent to the *quartiniers* of Paris to warn the people to be on their guard and to arm themselves, and then on Sunday between three and four o'clock in the morning, his Grace of Guise, his Grace of Aumale and others went to the Admiral's house, where the aforesaid Admiral was wounded with a boar-spear and thrown half-dead out of the window, and the Monday afterwards, having had his head removed, and his privities cut off by the little children, he was dragged belly-up by the said little children to the number of two or three hundred along the gutters of the city of Paris, as the ancient Romans did, who dragged tyrants *ad scalas gemonias unco*, the place of the Roman cloaca; and from there they went to hang the said Admiral up by his feet at Montfaucon. And it appears that God allowed all this because of the tyranny and the ill life of the aforesaid Admiral, who alone had been the author of the civil wars and the cause of the death of a hundred thousand men and the rape of girls, women and nuns and the sacking of the churches: and in short all lords should take warning from the example of this unhappy man that however much God may delay the punishment, it is all the worse for being deferred.

AN ACCOUNT OF COLIGNY'S MURDER, BY CAPTAIN STUDER VON
WINKELBACH, WHO COMMANDED THE DETACHMENT OF SWISS WHO BROKE
INTO THE ADMIRAL'S HOUSE.

Sunday, 24th August, was Saint Bartholomew's day. During the night the king said to his brother the duke of Anjou, 'Today, I want to prove that I am king of France; for until now, I have not been king. I want to be able to count the days of my reign from this day onwards.'

At about two in the morning he called for the palace guards, of whom a hundred belonged to him, the king, fifty-six to Anjou, and fifty to Alençon, who were in the plot, to make them take the oath and to await further orders on pain of corporal punishment.

Upon this, the Duke of Anjou took all the Swiss and the archers with him to lead them, at about five or six o'clock in the morning, to the admiral's house, for the Duke of Guise had deployed his men as if for battle.

The French then rushed the gates, which were defended by eight guards, who fought them and routed them and then closed the gates again. In the uproar one of them was killed.

The Swiss attacked the gates and beat them in with their halberds. The Duke of Guise called to those who were fighting in the lower part of the house to throw down their arms or they would all be run through.

When the Admiral's house was overrun, Moritz Grünenfelder of Niederuruen in the region of Glaris, was first into his room and he seized him, meaning to take him prisoner. At this Martin Koch of Freiburg, one of the Duke of Anjou's men, said to him, 'We are not ordered to do that.'

As the Admiral begged him to spare his old age, he thrust him through with the pike he was holding.

Captain Josué Studer of Saint Gall says that Moritz had found him standing up in his night-clothes and had led him to the light, saying, 'Knave, is it you?' And as it is said above, he ran the Admiral through with his halberd as he asked him to spare his old age. Presently the other also set upon him.

Guise asked if the Admiral were dead and that he should be thrown down into the street. As he struggled in his agony, he pushed his pike into his mouth. Then he was laid on the ground apart so that he could be recognised later.

LETTER FROM FATHER JOACHIM OPSER, S.J., SUB PRIOR OF THE COLLEGE OF CLERMONT, TO THE ABBOT OF SAINT GALL, DATED 26TH AUGUST, 1572

. . . Let me tell you more about the killing of the Admiral: I have these details from the man who struck the third blow with his battle-axe, Conrad Bürg, who was at one time groom to the bursar Joachim Waldemann, at Wyl. When the Swiss under the orders of the Duke of Anjou had broken down the doors, Conrad, followed by Leonhard Grünendfelder of Glaris and Martin Koch, reached the Admiral's room, which was the third in the house. First his servant was killed. The Admiral was in an ordinary dressing-gown and at first no one chose to lay hands on him; but Martin Koch, bolder than the others, struck the wretch with his battle-axe. Conrad gave him the third blow and at last, at the seventh, he fell dead against the fireplace by his room. By order of the Duke of Guise his body was thrown out of the window, and when they had put a rope round his neck as for a criminal they dragged him to the Seine, displaying him as a sight to the people. Such was the end of this pernicious man, who not only brought so many to the edge of the abyss during his lifetime, but in dying carried a crowd of heretical nobles down with him to hell . . .

The whole hog

In this last section you will be required to use all the skills you have acquired in the long slog so far. Now you will be expected to write some history – some carefully considered, well-grounded explanatory statements about the past.

1 Look at photograph **a)** and poem **b)**. Using evidence from both sources, write a brief historical statement about the role of racialism in British imperialism in the 1930s. Look up what you like in books, but what you say has got to be *your* statement, based on *this* evidence.

2 Look at the letter in section two. Did you know Britain once invaded Argentina? You learn a little every day. Use your skills in deciphering bad spelling and grammar and yourself write a perfectly constructed paragraph in matchless prose on the conditions of life of the British soldier in the early 19th century. (Same rules apply as above.)

3 This one will test your skills of scanning a long document! Read it to find 18th century attitudes to women. Don't let one morsel drop, however, get *all* of the evidence. Then turn it into a beautiful and powerful statement – my you *are* getting good!

4 Look at the letters in this the very last unit – deciphering again, and reading a whole lot, and looking for attitudes, and having to write superb history – all in one exercise. Don't go on strike, do it. Write a piece on the education of princes in early Tudor England – and make it good.

Now you are ready to get an A in your exam.

In September 1931 Gandhi came to London to attend the second India Round Table Conference in London. He made few concessions, least of all to the climate, as picture **1a)** shows. A year later a delegation of white farmers from Kenya came to ask for reduction of taxation. The Secretary of State refused to consider their case until they had withdrawn threats of unconstitutional action. The poem **1b)** appeared in a Kenyan newspaper. How do these documents demonstrate the problems inherent in the British Empire at this time?

80

1a)

1b)
You delegates that travelled hence
From Unofficial Conference
To lay its views before the great
And noble Secretary of State,
And for this purpose flew so far,
Whoever do you think YOU are?
How can you think that he'd be moved
By those whose loyalty is proved?
It's not as if there is a war
The nation might require you for.
By Jove, you fellows have a nerve!
What have you done that you deserve
A hearing? Have you tried to reach
Millions with rank seditious speech?
What efforts have you ever made
To interfere with British trade?
And what disturbance caused, of note?
Where are your loin cloths? Where's your goat?
Where is the ghostly toothless smile
And most unprepossessing dial,
Like that which charmed the public so
Not very many years ago?
You can't expect to air your views
As though you had been born Hindus:

       Kenya Karols, Carl C. Bourrie, Nakuru

81

The following letter was written by Private George Bee, shortly after the madcap expedition to Buenos Aires in 1807 (published in *Lincolnshire Life*, April 1983). How might the letter be used to comment on the condition of the British soldier at that time?

2   Dear Brother I right theas few lines to you hoping my mother and brother and sisters and all thar family is well as it levas me it present, thanks be to God for it. William Bee, I Hopes you will Remember me to all my (?) frends. I thanks God for my Retorn from Bunasayries for we have ben thro a Deal of Harchips for we was 9 munth on Bord of Ship Before whe went a Shore. The first Land we mad was the hialnd of Saint Jaggo in the West Eindes. Thear we stoped 1 munth and the Pepoll was all Black and nothing to cover they privats. Then we set siall and crost the Lion on the 29 of March wear the Sun is Right up and Down and not a Bet of Shader to be seen and we was Burnt to Death a most. The nex land we made was the Cape of Good Hope. It was a very fine place. I was a shore too Days. We stop 1 fornit and got water and privson for 1 munth then we set siall to Santellener wear the East Eindes Companys was, & stops 1 wek there set siall to Cape Sant Maray. Thear we see the south of Miacrikeray. We Cast Hanker 6 Days. A storm ros & lasted 4 days and nights. But with the Blessing of God it seas. We siall up the River Plat and lande ouer tropes on the 28 of jun without the Los of 1 man. On the 29 we march up to the medel in slug and water a Bout 6 miels, we march 7 days and without Braid or liquers. On the 3 of Jully we ingages the Enimeney and Drove them in to the Town that night, and we had a Rever to Cros and ide was O Blight to go up to the Nek in water and sum of the men was left beind, the Spanums cut thar ears of and thar hands by the rist and left them in thar Misery. On the 5th of Jully we storm the Town with the naked Banat, a Bout alf past 5 O Clock. Thar Strits was lind with Cannon. We drove the Enemeny from that part of the Town in to the Marctplace and Capthured part of the Town. That strong Battray wat tha Call the Bull Ring close to the Rever sied. As we went Down the Strets the Pepell was upon that House firing hat us; as we went down the Stret the Compney as I Blong ad very Bad Luck, for we lost 23 men the forst fier Jos Horton Wife Brother was wounded and he was my Left and man. John Woker was my Right and man. He was kill a Bout 12 O clock in the morning but he had very bad luck. General Craford got taken prisners and the Light Bagges. When we got in the Town we tokn no prisoner, kill all Before us. The dead Bodeys lies in the Streets as thik as tha cod lie.

Bunosayrirs was a strong place. The Houes was strang Belt, for we cod not Break in (?) theam, was Blight to fier in the dors tow or three tims before tha wold fli hopen and a nubber of women and children was kill that Day.

A flag of truth com from the Spanish General for a Season so ther was no more filing. We stoped 1 weak in the Bull Ring of Bunosayires. we toke on the 12 of Jully and set siall to Montovedo: thear we got Privsns for 6

82

munth. We stop a Bout 6 weks in Montovedo and set fire to all the shipping that we (?) got a wea. We lost two ships as we crost the Lin of the several Lincolnshire but non that com near Heignginton, but I see William Gosbey when we landed in the South of Meacirkerey. So no mor from your loving Brother

George Bee

John Woker com from Stanton (i.e. Stainton) near Langworth his father a farmer Rit by the torn of y post.

A certificate that accompanies the letters shows that George Bee was examined at the Royal Hospital, Chelsea on 27th August 1816. He was then an out-pensioner. He was 46, 5 foot 6 inches, brown hair, grey eyes, brown complexion, and 'rendered incapable of further service by Pulmonia and worn out from length of service. He is to reside in Lincoln.'

There follows an extensive letter of advice from Sir Charles Hotham to his daughter in 1769. Read it with care and then try to draw a word-picture of father and daughter. Then, bearing these in mind, use the letter to comment on the attitude to marriage of the eighteenth century gentleman. You might like to know that in fact the recipient never did marry . . .

3   MY DEAR HARRIET,

As you are now verging upon your 16th year, you are proceeding with hasty strides to make your entrance upon the great Stage of Life; and tho' the longer you can defer your appearance there, the more it will essentially be to your advantage, yet I think it high time, even thus early, to treat you as a Woman, that you may be the less at a loss how to play your part there, whenever you may be called upon so to do.

I consider you therefore no longer a child; and, indeed, since I have had, jointly with your Mother, the superintendency of your Education and Conduct, I have avoided doing so as much as possible, in order the sooner, by shaking off the follies, Prejudices and little Passions of Childhood, to open and enlarge your Mind and to ripen and direct your Judgment. To that end I have treated you always rather as my Younger Sister than my Daughter; and tho' it was highly improper to allow you to mix in the World, yet, as is common with Young People at that time of Life, I never shut you up in your Nursery, but made you my Companion; nay more, far from Secluding you from the Society and Conversation of my Friends and Acquaintances, I constantly encouraged you in becoming part of the Company. . . . It is natural for Youth to be more attentive to what is said of others than of themselves; and it saved me very often the disagreable task of harsher admonitions; not that it prevented them altogether, for sometimes, tho' not so frequently as they otherwise must have been, they were essentially necessary. However I trust and believe every thing of that sort is now over between us, and then I shall easily forget the pain they put me to, when I reflect you have reason to consider them as the only Remedy I could employ, and therefore the highest Obligation I could confer upon you.

Another reason I had, and a material one: that the more I seemingly left you to yourself, the less you would be upon your Guard, and that consequently I might the more easily see thro' your failings and inadvertancies. I will therefore endeavour in the course of what I shall say to you, to give you as perfect an account of yourself as I can, by setting up to you a Glass wherein you shall see the inmost part of you. If you like the Picture, or what you like of it, you will own and adopt as yours. If you dislike it altogether, you will destroy it and sit again, or you will blot out such parts as offend you, till you have obtain'd one quite to your mind. . . . But do not from hence be afraid I am going to preach you a Sermon, or enforce such rigid Doctrines as Youth and Gaiety must reject. I am going to do no such thing. Austerity is not consonant to my way of thinking. I would have you by all means enjoy the pleasures fitting for you, but I would wish you knew how to choose them; and that I might see that you govern'd *them*, not that they govern'd *you*. . . .

The Natural Walk and Situation of Woman, is Marriage. It will of Course be yours in common with the rest of your Sex, but when I sit down and consider that State in itself, and when I look Round me and see how few, how very few, become it, how Seldom their Chains, tho' golden ones, sit easy upon them, I tremble for you; It is of all others the most fiery trial you can undergo, and yet, as in all human probability you will attempt it, It is my Duty as far as I am able to point out to you the Variety of Rocks, Shoals, and Dangers in Short of all sorts, that you must encounter before you reach the Port, to which my infinite Affection for you will be your Pilot, and will endeavour to conduct you safely, if Possible, thro' them all.

The first object then that necessarily occurs both to your Mind and mine, is the choice of the Man with whom you are not only to pass your Life, but to whom you are to devote the whole of that Life. Upon that Choice depends your all; your Fame, Fortune, Person, Health, Happiness, or Misery; and as if this were not a Stake sufficient for one cast, there is Superadded to it the feelings of your Parents and Friends, as well as the Welfare or Wretchedness of your Children; for so far does this first irrecoverable false Step extend, as to affect not only those who have lived, but also Generations unborn. It has a Restrospect to the past, is decisive of the present, and carries with it that determinate property even to futurity. And since this is the light, and the true one, in which this important Step must be viewed, it behoves you to consider it well: but should you think, which perhaps you may, I paint rather too Strong, I desire only you will read over now and then, always with attention, the Marriage Ceremony, and I believe you will no longer be of that Opinion. You will find he has by the Laws of God and Man an absolute right to your Obedience; that he is your Head, your Lord, and Master, and that you must be Subordinate to him in all things. Let us then see what are the requisites to fit any Man for such a Dominion, and how You are to be recompensed for having submitted to have him impose it upon you. And be not discouraged: you may, and God knows I hope you will, meet with a very ample reward for having thus resign'd to him your Liberty; but let me assure you that Reward, provided your choice is a good one, is more in your own Hands than his; that is, it depends most upon your own Conduct.

Your Birth, Fortune, Connexions, and Situation in Life are such as entitle you to reject with Scorn any and every Man who is not a Gentleman, and your Principles I persuade myself are so good, that you would abhor the thought of being the Wife of a Dishonourable Man, even tho' he were of the first Nobility of this Country. What your personal Qualifications will be, it is impossible to say, as People of your Age change daily. At present, I who see you with more partial Eyes than your Lover will do, but who will not flatter you so much, will tell you, they are rather for you than against you, and yet you have nothing on that score to be particularly vain of, but if you had, It is a thought will never, I hope, gain admittance into your mind. When I come to speak of it I will shew it you in its true Colours. The present point now is what have you a right to expect in return for your Birth, Fortune and Person, – none of them of the very first Class, indeed, but all of them sufficient to enable you to look rather above than below you? Why you have undoubtedly a right to a Gentleman with a good Estate. The Word *Gentleman* it is unnecessary to define, and a good Estate I will not fix down to a determinate Sum; but leave the precise Idea of the one and the other to your own Judgment hereafter. Just now it is enough to caution you against flinging yourself away; which you would do had your Husband neither Birth, or Fortune, which would be the Case too had he even the one without the other. You would blush for ever to be tied to a low man, and you would Starve with a Gentleman who could not maintain you; for your fortune, tho' more considerable than you had originally reason to expect, is not, however, sufficient for you both. Thus you see what are your Expectations, but perhaps, which I shall not be surprised at, you have more Ambition for yourself than I have for you. You think you will become a Coronet, it may be so; and I would as little advise you against it if I saw the bestower of it worthy of you in other respects, as I should counsel you to accept it if I thought that his only merit.

High rank, tho' a fortuitous Advantage, and of course what no Man can value himself upon, is undoubtedly a great one; for when it is supported with worth and Honour it is worn with a dignity and a real lustre that commands admiration and Respect, and if such you can find, Win it and wear it by all means. But if you so foolishly set your Heart upon it, as to seek it, you never will obtain it with that degree of Comfort and happiness attending it I wish you. Should it even fall in your way, distrust it, beware of it, be not dazzled with the Glare and Glitter of it, for be assured You have not so good a chance for solid Happiness with it as without it. The wretched Education of our Young Nobility in General but too much authorizes me to say so: there is scarce an Englishman among them; It is a Composition of Italien and French, awkwardly, and, what is worse, viciously put together. Their Life is consequently one continued Scene not of pleasure, – if it were I would forgive them, – but of dissipation, in which very creditable Amusement they waste their Time, their Health, their Fortune, their Parts, (if Providence had been so much kinder to them than they deserved as to bestow any upon them,) and their Character. Unless necessity obliges them to enter into the factious views of desining Men, they are dumb in the Senate, but petulantly loud at Almacks, and ignorantly and impertinently so every where else. From Men of such a cast, what are you to expect at home? A sullen morose Disposition, a total Negligence and Disregard of you, your Children, and all Domestic thoughts and Cares. I do not however, mean to say this is the Characteristick of all men of Quality; certainly there are many endued with many Virtues, and if it be your lot to fall into the hands of one of them, would to God He may be of the latter Class.

But rather than title, It is your Business to seek for good sense, good Nature, and Honour. If your Husband possesses these Qualities, it is your own fault if you are not a happy Woman. You will look up to him, and confide in him; and he will hold you up in the World in proportion to the Consequence he is of in it. If he be ten Years at least older than you, so much the better; You will have the Higher Opinion of his Judgment, and will with the greater Pleasure be guided by it. If you think more highly of his understanding than your own, You will have the fairest Prospect before you; but if on the contrary you in your own Mind give yours the preference, you are infallibly lost in his Esteem, and forfeit at once every view of Domestic Comfort.

I will now suppose the Man of your Choice is precisely what you wish, and what he ought to be; that his Opinion of you is great, and his Affection for you still greater; that you are consequently perfectly happy, and fully perswaded you shall be so for ever. Many Women have had equal reason to say, and have said the same thing, yet many have been, and are every Day, totally mistaken. Let us find out, if we can, from whence this arises.

One of the first causes of it, I take to be, that they set out originally wrong. They are so easily flatter'd, and find so much pleasure in so sensible a Gratification to their vanity, that they are too soon led to set a much higher value upon themselves than it is possible they can deserve, and thence unreasonably think this golden Dream is to last for ever; and when the Husband shews them it is time to lay aside the Mistress in order to assume the more respectable Character of Wife, Disappointment ensues, and in its train follows, Sulleness, Peevishness, Altercation, and all those petty Airs silly Women put on when they are hastening to their own undoing. Be you wise enough not to expect too much and you will avoid Mortification; trust in your Husband but distrust yourself; and Stifle in its Birth, as you would a Serpent in your Bosom, every tincture of Vanity.

Shall I tell you I am afraid You are not quite exempt from it, but sure you will be from henceforth everlastingly, when you consider it as it ought to be seen, in the meanest, lowest, and most Contemptible light. It is of all the silly Vices that assail and possess a female Mind unquestionably the most dangerous to her Character and peace of Mind; besides I do protest to you, I never knew any Individual Creature that was not essentially the worse for it. It leads into a thousand Scrapes and never yet got any body out of one. Affectation is a Spice of it, and so poor and insignificant a mockery of its execrable original, that it only renders the wearer of it compleatly ridiculous.

You have it not, I hope, but you have some times so much the Appearance of it that those who do not know you well, may mistake it. Can you then be too attentive to correct it?

Now if you have neither Vanity nor Affectation, your Mind and Temper will always be so entirely in its natural Seat, that you will at all times be prepared to meet your Husband with Smiles and Sunshine; and you are qualified hitherto so to do; for to do you justice I believe your Heart excellent, and your disposition to be both good temper'd, and good natured. You are from Constitution Chearful, and lively from good Spirits. They are a real Blessing, and, when properly conducted, of the greatest use; but while you Cherish them, take care they do not run away with you, which they are sometimes apt to do: they lead you insensibly to talk too much and too fast. It is a bad habit and gives every Woman who has it the Appearance of being either Silly, or forward, or both. Good Spirits are sometimes, tho' never by a discerning Eye, mistaken for Wit. But Wit at best is so dangerous a talent that I should be sorry you possessed it. It creates millions of Enemies, and never made a Friend. It is a two edged Weapon, it cuts both ways: and I have often seen Women who thought themselves exceedingly Witty, when they were only abusive, scurrilous, and Impudent.

Take care of being too Volatile; it unsettles and unhinges the mind, and renders it incapable of attention to any thing. It suffers nothing to make that Impression it should, and I have seen you often from thence tho' fully perswaded of the truth and consequence of what has been said to you at the time, shake it off the next Instant, and think no more of it a second time than if it had never happen'd. That you should totally alter in this particular is of the utmost and Deepest Importance to you; for what Confidence can any Man have in any Woman who pays with him, and yet in practice disregard the next moment every thing he has, for her good, and perhaps necessarily for his own sake too, given himself the trouble to say to her? She cannot expect he will ever forgive such an unpardonable Inattention.

That you may then the better study, with effect, your Husband's Temper and Disposition, (which if you do not do and conform to it too minutely, you will be miserable,) It is necessary You should turn your Eye upon

Yourself, and be fully apprized of your own, that you may correct those imperfections (the condition of human nature), that are, and must be, perpetually arising. It is what every wise Woman, and Man too, must do continually.

You are quick and Hasty enough to be sometimes look'd upon as passionate, which to speak of it in the gentlest terms is a very great Inconvenience. I am sorry you possess it in the smallest degree, because I know by my own experience how much it ought to be avoided. I am unfortunately extremely passionate naturally, but by infinite Attention and Care have been happy enough so far to have Corrected it that I do not recollect to have ever suffer'd from it essentially; and I promise you I should not have got thro' Life as I have done had I not got the better of myself even as I have, which I confess is by no means sufficient. I beg you to remember You are never upon an account whatever, notwithstanding any provocation you may receive, to let a hasty word, much less an angry Passionate Expression, escape your Lips towards your Husband.

I have seen about you, when you have been told of a fault, I will not call it Obstinacy, but a Resistance that, unless You resolve to check it, will too soon become so: and think of the Folly of it: for to what end can a Wife possibly be Obstinate, when she knows, if he chooses She should, she must submit.

I do not mention any one of these things, either to put you out of humour with yourself, or me, but meerly to keep my word with you in shewing You Yourself. I do not upbraid you with your Mistakes, I will not call them Faults; all I mean is to point them out to you that you may know them; for unless you do, It cannot be expected you should amend them.

If therefore You receive this as coming from a rigid Monitor and not from your best Friend, you do me the highest Injustice, and are your own worst Enemy.

I will take it for granted then that You see and feel your Errors and imperfections, and are fully resolved to the utmost of your power to correct them all; nay I will go farther, that you actually have done so; therefore what follows will be chiefly to your Conduct, rather than to your Failings.

And that it may be at all times such as must be productive of many Virtues, accustom yourself to think of the part you are to bear in marriage, not in a frightful Point of View, but in a most serious one, for it well deserves that Consideration: and lay it down as a principle in your own mind never to be departed from, that there is nothing in it indifferent, nothing trivial, but that every thing is of Consequence.

The first thing you have to do is to gain your Husband's good opinion; that once settled, you may make yourself sure of his esteem, Friendship, and Affection, and the primary Ingredient towards obtaining and retaining them, is to have a due Sense of Religion, and to be uniform, constant, and firm in the Practice, and Exercise of it. It is the Bond of Peace, and the

Source of every virtue. I need, I am sure, say no more upon this great Point, because I am happy in believing you think and act in that respect as you ought, not meerly from [having] been told from your Childhood it is right, but because you feel in your Heart it is so. Besides, it softens and gives to the mind such a Constant Serenity as will prevent your ever appearing with a cloud on your Brow.

The Cares, Anxieties, and Business of the World, may often have that effect upon him; and whenever they have, It is your Part never to see it or enquire into the Cause of it, but with Gentleness and good humour, two Lenitives you always have in your Power, to endeavour to alleviate it. If he thinks proper to trust you with it, you will know what to do; but never attempt to learn what he chooses to conceal, and never fancy yourself the Object of his displeasure till he informs you you are so. I know many Women who imagine this perpetual Sollicitude about themselves is a proof of their Affection; It is no such thing; it arises from Curiosity and Vanity, either of which are sufficient to fret, teaze, and wear any reasonable Man to Death.

It was well said by Madame de Maintenon to the Duchess of Burgundy, let your Husband be your only Confidant and your First Friend: but let me add to it, tho' you are never to have a Secret from him, you should never pry into his.

You would have, if you encouraged it, and practice will do so, a turn for Play; lay it down then for a Rule never to Play but merely for amusement, and rather to oblige other People than yourself; and then for such trifling Sums as make it a matter of meer indifference to you whether you win or lose. The moment your Mind becomes so far engaged as to make you eager about it, It ceases to be an amusement, but is a serious pursuit that, if you follow it, cannot fail of making your seriously miserable. But could no greater mischief arise from it than to so put you off your Guard as to make you lose your Temper, is not that enough? Does it not cost you the Best thing about you? And I ask you, if even in your observation, you ever saw a number of People at play, tho' for what could not materially affect them, without some of them exposing themselves extremely?

I have never let slip an Opportunity of inculcating in you the Necessity of Cleanliness, in your Person, Dress, and general Appearance; and I have labour'd this essential Point with you upon all Occasions, because I knew the extreme Consequence of it, which you do not seem to do; for you are inclined, either from Indolence or Hurry, to be much too negligent in that Particular. I cannot Conceive what merit you find in being dirty and a Slatern, or where you learnt it; not from your Mother I am sure, for she is as much the reverse as any Woman can be, and so I hope will you. I say this, as I perceive with great Pleasure you are forsaking so filthy a Habit. Besides its being filthy, there is Shocking Indecency in it that, believe me, no Man can endure. No Woman who values her own happiness, or her Husband's affection, will ever for an Instant appear in his Sight undressed;

(and I recommend to your Serious reading a very true and a very pretty Paper upon this Subject in the Spectator,) much less dirty, in the most trifling instance, must she be, unless she means to disgust him for ever.

Cleanliness, as it is a principal Ornament, so it is the first beauty; and it is amazing every Woman has it not, for it is in every Woman's power: if She wishes to please she cannot succeed more effectually, especially with her Husband, than by doing the thing in the World perhaps the most agreable to him and comfortable to herself. Another great Advantage it has is, that it is a Strong Index of Purity of Mind as well as manners, It is the Height of Elegancy and good Breeding, and Strongly marks out the fruit of a good Education and the Character of a Gentlewoman. And such a Woman ought constantly to appear with that Freshness about her that is ascribed to Venus rising out of the Sea, not that she need go so far to answer that End. Water is to be had in profusion in every House and should be used accordingly; to shew the Veneration our Forefathers had for ablutions, Bathing was made one of the first articles of Religion, and most wisely so, as nothing contributes more to Health. It continues to be so in some Sects to this Day, as even with us in the Article of Baptism.

Upon every account, a Woman who feels her own dignity as a rational Creature, will dare to defy the searching penetrating Eye of the Microscope. Her dress will be as clean as her Person, but if that is not so to the nicest, minutest, degree, no matter what it is cover'd with, one dirty rag will do as well as another. If it is, what you wear is not indifferent. All Men Love to see Women they are so nearly connected with well dress'd; that is, that what they put on should be good of its kind, and well chosen. I would even, if your Husband did not disapprove of it and that your Circumstances admitted of it, recommend it to you, not to be Gaudily and Magnificently Deck'd out, but to be rather fine than otherwise. Without all your attention to this Requisite you must never expect to see your Children, or Servants, or House in order. They will take their Impressions from you; and you will be the Pendulum to regulate, direct, and ascertain their Motions in this as in every thing else.

No Woman ever had ONE QUARREL ONLY with her Husband, many I hope never had one, and I flatter myself you will be of that Number; but from the beginning of time to this Hour, the first Quarrel never was the last. Avoid it by every possible means as you would the plague. Never enter into an argument with him, no matter how serious or how trifling the subject, it must beget Warmth, which will produce dispute, which can only end in a Quarrel, in which you must infallibly be in the Wrong because it is your part, Business, and Duty, to submit. He will no doubt have failings like other men; you must expect it and be prepared for it; and do not foolishly imagine you are to reclaim him by Argument or tears. He will think you impertinent in the first Case, and weak in the Second. You must be Deaf, Dumb, and Blind to them all, whatever they may be; there is your only Remedy, and, depend upon it, It will not prove a fruitless one; Time and Reflexion will bring about what Reproaches and Lamentations would never effect; and your Patience, Meekness, and Forebearance will, in Spite of himself, force him back to you with ten times more Affection and Love than perhaps he ever possessed.

Treat his Friends as you would your own, and make them so if you can: you will find your account in it; for they will insensibly raise you in his Opinion. He will be sensibly flatter'd with their Approbation of his Choice, and certainly Love you the better for it, and you will please and oblige him in the highest degree by every attention you can shew them. Receive them always, no matter how inconveniently they come, with open arms. Who do you think would bear to see his Friend or even Common Acquaintance, coldly treated or Slighted in his House?

As to your own Friends, the fewer you have the better. Intimacies between Women are in general dangerous things. They are too apt to form them too lightly, and to break them with as little cause. They fancy themselves at first, and at once, perfectly Sincere, whereas that they are but weak quickly manifests itself in the Discovery of each other's little Secrets, and then their Simple Quarrels become the amusement of the Town, and they the ridicule of it; for, be assured, and I believe you have seen Instances of this Truth, no Mortal pities them, or indeed cares one farthing about them.

Treat your Servants with the greatest mildness, and goodness: reward and encourage those who are good; and dismiss immediately those who prove otherwise; and tho' you must necessarily have more trust and confidence in some than in others, yet there is no occasion any should be too great Favourites or treated with an improper Familiarity. You will be the Happier if they are not, and so will they; as no sensible Servant who knows his own Interest will wish it; and Regularity, Economy, Order, and Subordination, (which you must insist upon without relaxation) will be the consequence of it, and will give you the best Chance you can have for Quiet and good Humour.

As to the Domestic Affairs of your Family, take as much of them upon yourself, readily and chearfully as your Husband may choose you should: look upon it as it is, one of your principal Duties; and attend to it assiduously. Never suppose it an Object below your notice, or beneath your care; for besides that it must be an infinite Satisfaction to you to lessen and take off so much of his trouble, It is an Occupation exceedingly honourable to you, and an amusement infinitely more solid, and therefore greater, than any You can meet with abroad: for there is nothing more certain that however a Woman may please abroad, It is at Home only she Shines. Make that Home, therefore, for your own Sake and your Husband's, by every means you can conceive, as agreable to him as possible; let him see you always happy there, and pleased with his Company and Conversation, and with that of his Friends; and to fit Yourself to bear a becoming part in his and their Society, Study to improve your understanding to the very best of your power and abilities; if you do not, and can only talk of Fanns and Tippets, and repeat over the Chit Chat, News, and Scandal of the Day, you will soon perceive he does not think you a Companion for him. Take up always the turn of the Discourse, but never give it: and never suppose that in order to appear pleased you are always to talk, or always to laugh, It is a tiresome, Wearing, idle Habit and is excessively Ill bred. Talking at random will keep him in a Fever while he loves you, and will make him despise you when he does not. I do not mean you should be quite Silent, and, like the Children, never speak but when you are Spoke to, but I would have you accustom yourself to have a constant guard upon yourself in that respect, which if it does not make you say a good thing (which, by the bye, it *will*), certainly will prevent your saying a silly one; or what you may ever have reason to repent of. Recollect that the emptiest Vessels sound always the loudest; and then I think you never can give into that rage for talking, and Intemperance of Tongue that is really intolerable. Besides, the highest good manners is to give every body their Share, not run away with it all oneself; and it is the greatest Instance of good Sense to act an underpart. Mankind will always give you credit for what you do not assume; and send but People away satisfied with themselves, and you may depend upon their being pleased with you.

I have said enough in this large Field I have enter'd into to induce you to behave to your Husband with Attention, Civility, which no Familiarity should ever destroy, and Respect. That should Constantly be your Conduct in publick and in private; and you depart from Decency, Delicacy, and your Dignity, if ever you manifest towards him before any human Eye the least faimilar Fondness; it would be disgusting to him, and Shocking to every body else.

And now I think it is time I should dismiss you and relieve myself. I have given you the best advice I can, and I can only say the more of it you follow the happier Woman you will be. Receive it therefore as I meant it, give it fairly your Attention, and I think your Heart will tell you to pursue it. If you do, I do not doubt of its having the Effect I earnestly wish it may, and then I shall feel the trouble is has cost me to be the pleasantest act of my Life.

The documents given below all relate to the education of important young people in the reign of Henry VIII. They are taken from Henry Ellis's *Original Letters*. Letter **a)** is from Richard Croke, the Duke of Richmond's schoolmaster, to Cardinal Wolsey. The Duke of Richmond was the illegitimate but much loved son of Henry VIII. Letters **b)** and **d)** come from Henry Dowes, schoolmaster to Gregory Cromwell, son to the King's chief minister, Thomas Cromwell. Letter **c)** is from Gregory to his father. Read them through and then use the evidence they contain to draw up a brief statement of the problems of tutors of rich and important children in this period.

4a) Moste humbely besechith your Grace your Orator and daylie bedeman Richard Croke scole master to the duke of Richmonde, that yt wolde please your Grace of your most habundant goodnes to directe yor most gracius lettres of comaundment unto my Lord of Richemonds Counsell comprysing these Articles followinge.

Ffirst the quantytie of tyme which I shall dayle occupie with my Lorde in lerenynge by your Grace appoyntid, the said Councell parmyt and suffer me to have accesse unto hym oone hower before masse and brekefast accordynge to your Grace's former comaundemente. The rest of the tyme of ynstruccyon of my saide Lorde to be taken at my discression, and as I shall parceyve most convenyent; and my saide Lorde moste apte to Lerne. Provided that no more tyme by me be occupied in oone daye then be your Grace shalbe appoyntid. Ne that I so remytt eny parte of the same, that thereby my Lordes lernynge may decay.

Seconde that where as my said Lorde is forced to wryte of his owen hande to abbotts and meane parsons contrary to your Grace's comaundment; and that ymedyatly after his dynner and repast taken; to the grete dullynge of his wytts sprytes and memory, and no litell hurte of his hed, stomak, and body; and that yt were very necessary in my pore judgement my said Lorde shuld wryte noo thyng of his owen hande but in Latten specially to the Kyngs Highnes and your moste noble Grace, to thentent he myght more fermely imprynte in his mynde both wordes and phrases of the Latten tonge, and the soner frame hym to some good stile in wrytinge whereunto he is now very rype;yt wolde please your Grace therefore to determyn and appoynte both certayne persons, and also certayne tymes in the weke, to whome only, and when, my said Lorde shall wryte either in Englishe or in the Latten tonge, as your high wisdom shall thinke moste convenyente. Provided the said exersise of his handle and stile in both the tonges be commytted oonly to the discression and ordre of me his scole master: and that no man may force hym to wryte oonles I be there presente, to dyrecte and forme his said hande and stile.

Thirdely that where as by example of good education, as well as noryture as good lernying, of suche yonge gentilmen as by your Graces comaundement be attendant upon my said Lorde, the same myght more facyly be induced to profit in his lerenynge, yt wolde please your Grace to gyve comaundemente that the Instruction of the said gentilmen be at the only order and diposicion of the scole master, so that they be streytely comaundid to applye their lernynge at such tymes as I shall thinke conuenient without mayntenaunce of eny man to the contrary. And also that none of them ne any other be sufferid to contynue in my lordes chamber durynge the tyme of his lernynge, but such only as the said scole master shall thinke mete for the furtherance of the same.

Ffourthly, yt wolde please your Grace in likewise to comande that the tyme of my lordes lernynge by yor Grace appoyntid be not interupted for euery tryefull, or resorte of euery stranger, but only strangers of honor, to whome also if my said lorde myght by the advise of his Scolemaster exhibit and make som shew of his lernyng, like as he was wont and doth of his other pastymes, it shulde greately enourage hym to his lernyng; to the which, bycause it is moste laborious and tedyous to children, his Grace shulde be moste specially anymated and encoraged.

Ffynally, that no wayes, color, ne crafte be taken to discorage, alyenate, or averte my said lordss mynde from lernyng, or to extyncte the love of lernynge in his estymacion, but that he be induced most highly to esteme his boke of all his other studies. The which thing with other the premisses obteyned, I dare be bolde to assure your Grace that his lernyng at the sight of your Grace shall with no litel tyme, and much pleasure of hymselff, farr surrmounte and passe the knowledge of his yeres, tyme, and age, noone excepte.

4b) PLEASITH it your Maistershipp to be advertised that Mr Gregory with all his companie here ar (thankes be to God) in healthe; daylie occupied and embusied in the treyne and exercice of lerninge; under such maner and forme as there is no small hope the successe therof to be suche as shall contente and satisfie your good truste and expectation, beinge moche more lykelehodde of proffecte and encrease then att any tyme hertofore, partely for cause he is now brought sumewhat in an awe and dreade redy to gyve himself to studie when he shalbe therunto requyred, and partelie sithens thinges whiche hertofore have alienated and detracted hys mynde from labours to be taken for th'attaignement of good lettres are now subdued and withdrawne, wherunto (as a thinge nott of leste momente and regarde) may be addyde the ripenes and maturitie of his wytte; whiche nott beinge of that hasty sorte that by and by do bringe forth theire frute, doth dailie growe to a more docilitie and apte redines to receyve that that shalbe shewyd him by his teachers. The order of his studie, as the houres lymyted for the Frenche tongue, writinge, plaienge att weapons, castinge of accomptes, pastimes of instruments, and suche others, hath bene devised and directed by the prudent wisdome of Mr Southwell; who with a ffatherly zeale and amitie muche desiringe to have hime a sonne worthy

94

suche parents, ceasseth not aswell concerninge all other things for hime mete and necessary, as also in lerninge, t'expresse his tendre love and affection towardes hime, serchinge by all meanes possible howe he may moste proffitte, dailie heringe hime to rede sumwhatt in thenglishe tongue, and advertisenge hime of the naturell and true kynde of pronuntiacon therof, expoundinge also and declaringe the etimologie and native signification of suche wordes as we have borrowed of the Latines or Frenche menne, not evyn so comonly used in our quotidiene speche. M^r. Cheny and M^r. Charles in lyke wise endevoireth and emploieth themselves, accompanienge M^r. Gregory in lerninge, amonge whome ther is a perpetuall contention, strife, and conflicte, and in maner of an honest envie who shall do beste, not oonlie in the ffrenche tongue (wherin M^r. Vallence after a wonderesly compendious, facile, prompte, and redy waye, nott withoute painfull delegence and laborious industrie doth enstructe them) but also in writynge, playenge at weapons, and all other theire exercises, so that if continuance in this bihalf may take place, whereas the laste Diana, this shall (I truste) be consecreted to Apollo and the Muses, to theire no small profecte and your good contentation and pleasure. And thus I beseche the Lord to have you in his moste gratious tuition. At Reisinge in Norff the last daie of Aprill.

Your faithfull and most bounden servaunte

HENRY DOWES.

4c) RIGHT worsehypfull father, I comend me un to you, desyryng you of youre dayly blessyng, sartyfying you that I am in good helth, wyth my cosens Bersfourd and Wellyfyd, thanks be unto God omnipotente, and apply owre boks dylygently, as shall appere I trust to youre worschyp and owre proffyts. Father, I besetch you whan ye mett wyth the ryght honorable lorde of Oxforth, to geue thanks un to hys Lorchyp, for whan he came to a towne callyd Yeldam, to the parsons there of to hunte the foxe, he sente for me and my cossyns, and mad us good schere; and lett us see schuch game and plesure as I never saye in my lyfe; more over father, I besetch you to geve thanks to the for sayde parson of Yeldam, which sens I came in to the cuntry hath dyvers tymys sente for me and for my cossyns and mad us hygh schere, and schewyd us gret plesure. For all other thyngs consarnyng my rayment, I beseche you geve credens to my synguler good frende Mayster doctor Lee. Thus Jhesu have you in hys kepyng. From Topsfyld the xvii day of October. By your lowly sone

GREGORY CRUMWELL

4d) AFTER that it pleased your Maistershipp to give me in charge not onlie to give diligent attendaunce uppon Maister Gregory, but also to instructe hime with good lettres, honeste maners, pastymes of instrumentes, and suche other qualities as sholde be for hime mete and conveniente, pleasith it you to understande that for the accomplishement therof I have

95

indevoured myself by all weys possible to invent and excogitate howe I might moste profett hime, in whiche bihalf thorowgh his diligence the successe is suche as I truste shalbe to your good contentation and pleasure, and his no smale profecte. But forcause somer was spente in the servyce of the wylde goddes it is so moche to be regarded after what fashion yeouth is educate and browght upp, in whiche tyme that that is lerned (for the moste parte) will nott all holelie be forgotten in the older yeres, I thinke it my dutie to asserteyne yor Maistershippe how he spendith his tyme, so that if there be any thinge contrary your good pleasure, after advertisement receyved in that bihalf it may be amended. And firste, after he hath herde Masse he taketh a lecture of a Diologe of Erasmus Colloquium, called Pietas puerilis, whereinne is described a veray picture of oone that sholde be vertuouselie brought upp, and forcause it is so necessary for hime I do not onelie cause him to rede it over, but also to practise the preceptes of the same, and I have also translated it into Englishe, so that he may conferre theime both to githers, wherof (as lerned men affirme) cometh no small profecte; whiche translation pleasith it you to receyve by the bringer herof, that ye may judge howe moche profitable it is to be lerned: after that, he exerciseth his hande in writing one or two houres, and redith uppon Fabian's Chronicle as longe; the residue of the day he doth spende uppon the lute and virginalls. When he rideth (as he doth very ofte) I tell hime by the way some historie of the Romanes or the Greekes, whiche I cause him to reherse agayn in a tale. For his recreation he useth to hawke and hunte, and shote in his long bowe, which frameth and succedeth so well with hime that he semeth to be therunto given by nature. My Lorde contineweth, or rather daily augmenteth his goodnes towardes hime. Also the gentle men of the country, as Sir John Dawne, Sir Henry Delves, M^r. Massey, M^r. Brereton baron of the Kinges Escheker there, and diverse other so gently hath interteigned hime that they seme to strive who shold shew hime moste pleasures; of all whiche thinges I thowght it my dutie to asserteigne your good Maistershipp, most humblie desirenge the same to take in good parte this my rude boldnes. And thus I pray the Trinitie longe to preserve yor good health with encrease of moche hono^r. At Chester the vjth daie of Septembre.

Your humble servaunte
HENRY DOWES.

To his moste worshipfull Maister
  Mr Secretaire.

List of documents

1 October 1945; **2** June 1939; **3** January 1944; **4** October 1945; **5** January 1944; **6** January 1939; **7** January 1944; **8** October 1945; **9**, **10**, **11**, June 1939; **12** October 1945; **13** May 1940; **14** October 1945; **15** January 1944; **16** January 1939

Acknowledgements

The author and publishers would like to thank the following for permission to reproduce material in this book:

Mary Evans Picture Library (cover photograph)

The *Guardian* (p. viii); *Sussex Express and County Herald* and Leigh Photographic/Leigh Simpson (p. 40); *The Times* (pp. 41–42); The Bowes Museum, Co Durham (pp. 44–45); Barnardo Photo Archive (p. 50); The Smithsonian Institution (p. 51); Hereford and Worcester County Council (p. 65); George Wain/The National Trust (p. 66); BBC Hulton Picture Library (p. 67); The Bodley Head Ltd: *St Bartholomew's Night* by Philippe Erlanger (p. 71); BBC Hulton Picture Library (p. 81); *Lincolnshire Life* 9 (p. 82).